F. WARREN MCFARLAN

EFFECTIVE FUNDRAISING

THE TRUSTEE'S ROLE AND BEYOND

Foreword by Abby Falik

WILEY

Library of Congress Cataloging-in-Publication Data
Names: McFarlan, F. Warren (Franklin Warren), author.
Title: Effective fundraising : the trustees role and beyond / F. Warren McFarlan.
Description: Hoboken, New Jersey : Wiley, [2021] | Includes bibliographical references and index.

Identifiers: LCCN 2020046372 (print) | LCCN 2020046373 (ebook) |
ISBN 9781119772286 (cloth) | ISBN 9781119772309 (adobe pdf) |
ISBN 9781119772293 (epub)

Subjects: LCSH: Trusts and trustees. | Fund raising. | Nonprofit organizations.
Classification: LCC HD62.6 .M386 2021 (print) | LCC HD62.6 (ebook) |
DDC 658.15/224--dc23

LC record available at https://lccn.loc.gov/2020046372
LC ebook record available at https://lccn.loc.gov/2020046373

Cover Design: Wiley
Cover Image: © ONYXprj/Getty Images

SKY10025040_021721

This book is dedicated to
Professor Herman B. Leonard,
Professor Kasturi Rangan,
and
Eliot I. Snider,
Social Enterprise Pioneers.

Contents

Foreword

Shortly after graduating from business school, I launched Global Citizen Year, the nonprofit social enterprise I've grown and led since 2010. At Global Citizen Year, we're pioneering a new pathway between high school and college—one that wraps coaching and curriculum around real-world experience, to unlock curiosity, conviction, and courage in our next-generation leaders. From the beginning, a core pillar of our mission has been to ensure access to exceptional young people who reflect our society's diversity. This commitment has required a significant need for philanthropy which, as Warren McFarlan so aptly notes, has meant over half my time (and, yes, "the harder half"!) has been focused on fundraising. To date, we've raised and deployed over $30 million in philanthropy. Of our 1,000 alumni, 80% have received some level of need-based financial aid and over 30% have participated on a fully funded scholarship.

None of this would have been possible without the commitment and engagement of my board. Along the way, I've learned a tremendous amount about how to support our trustees in supporting our mission, though much of what I've learned has been through trial and error. The beauty of Warren McFarlan's book is that it provides a blueprint for accelerating the learning curve for all of an organization's stakeholders.

This timely and practical book is a comprehensive guide for trustees—particularly those serving on the boards of well-established nonprofits with clear governance structures, broad networks of supporters, and a long history. These include colleges and universities, private schools, major hospitals, and arts institutions. For those interested in serving on the board of grass-roots or social-change organizations, Chapter 9 shares helpful advice about the role a board plays in supporting the unique challenges—and opportunities—of organizations that are younger, high-growth, and/or founder-led.

The book also outlines the broad range of roles trustees can play in contributing to the crucial function of fundraising. Time and again, I've found that people assume fundraising necessarily requires making direct asks, but this couldn't be further from the truth. While some (rare) souls are enthusiastic about directly soliciting gifts, others may prefer to play equally impactful roles—expanding networks, making introductions, lending credibility, or providing the coaching and context that contribute to a successful "close."

As we've built the board at Global Citizen Year, I've made a point of spending time with each prospective trustee to discuss the role s/he would most like to play in generating resources for the organization. We expect everyone to make a contribution that feels generous according to each person's means (as Warren McFarlan says, "giving enough that it hurts"), but recognize that the specific amount looks different for everyone.

Additionally, I ask each board member to identify the fundraising role each would get energy from: is it hosting a cocktail party or "friendraiser"? Making warm introductions to new prospects? Designing a viral marketing campaign? Accompanying me to meetings in person or (as of this writing in the time of Coronavirus Covid-19) via ZOOM? The key to successful engagement, in my experience, is finding the sweet spot between what the organization needs and what you—as trustee—can distinctively offer. Once we've defined your role, my job as CEO is to keep you motivated and equipped to play it successfully.

One of the other things the book does so well is to debunk the myth that fundraising is the dirty work of begging for resources. McFarlan writes, "You are not begging, but rather offering an unusual and attractive opportunity to the prospective donor to invest in their passion and to have their name associated with it long term." I couldn't agree more. My approach to fundraising changed fundamentally once I recognized that, to a high-net-worth individual looking to give away money, *I* was the one who brought the scarcer resource to the relationship—that is, a clear path to make a meaningful and distinctive impact in the world. No longer did I see myself pleading for support; instead I knew I was showing up with a valuable opportunity. This shift—along with the insight that the most successful fundraising must be relational, not transactional—has been a revelation for me, as well as for our board. Any time I hear a board member complain that they don't like asking for money, I remind them that it's a privilege to invite others to join us in a cause we believe in fiercely. This change in frame shifts the narrative from "I have to ..." to "I get to ..." and it makes a world of difference.

This book will help you find a cause you can't not do something about and a mission that, in the author's words, "you talk continuously about it to the point of driving people around you crazy." Once you've found it, you can look the CEO and your fellow trustees in the eye and say, "I see you. I trust you. Let's do this. How can I help?" And, you're off to the races.

I wish this book existed when I set out to found Global Citizen Year, and I'm so glad it now does. There's no doubt it will be a valuable guide in driving the resources that advance the causes you care most about. Ultimately, it's not just about the cash—it's about bfringing the credibility, candor, compassion, and commitment that will change the world. For good.

Abby Falik
Founder/CEO
Global Citizen Year

Preface

SOCIAL ENTERPRISE ORGANIZATIONS have played a vibrant and important role in the United States for the past century, encompassing nearly 15% of the workforce. These organizations have received deep and enduring support from philanthropy as they pursued their mission. My earliest memories include the kettles of the Salvation Army, the offering plates in church, and the extraordinary success of the 70,000-person organization The March of Dimes in the 1950s that funded the discovery of the Salk vaccine and the Sabin vaccine. These vaccines led to the elimination of the scourge of polio. This work has continued unabated until today with the research supporting cures for the Coronavirus Covid-19 being only the latest.

I have spent a large amount of my time working for a social enterprise and much of the rest of it serving on social enterprise boards over the past 40 years. It has been rich and exciting work. New transforming services have been launched and the world is much the better for them. It is both exciting and fun to design these new services. Not so much fun is designing a revenue model to work in tandem with the services to produce a viable organization.

In my previous book, *Joining a Nonprofit Board: What You Need to Know* with Marc Epstein, we placed a heavy focus on the board's role in defining mission, evolving mission, and understanding mission. In retrospect, we slid by too rapidly the fact that mission is sometimes deeply constrained/shaped by financial realities and must morph to deal with that reality.

This book is about development. In *Joining a Non-Profit Board: What You Need to Know*[1] we laid out three roles for the board of trustees:

1. The definition and approval of the organization's mission and the strategy to achieve it.
2. The selection, coaching, and evaluation of the CEO.
3. The securing of the necessary financial resources for the organization.

This book has focused on the third of these roles—the one that social enterprise CEOs repeatedly say consumes 50% of their time. Without funds, mission cannot be fulfilled. Development is the lifeblood of most social enterprises, be they large or small. It is the unique and special responsibility of its trustees and supporters to help secure resources for the organization. These resources are often critical to the organization's success, if not survival. There are many ways that individual trustees, given their resources and skill sets, can go about this task. Attracting and harnessing the energies of the right people is key to the long-term success of development.

Without a sustainable revenue model, even the most exciting mission-driven organization will collapse. Repeatedly, my social enterprise CEO friends say that over half their lives (and the harder half) are focused on fundraising. The dirty truth is with no fundraising, there is no social enterprise or enduring mission.

---

[1] Marc J. Epstein and F. Warren McFarlan, *Joining a Nonprofit Board: What You Need to Know* (John Wiley & Sons, 2011).

This book is focused squarely on that reality: Asking for Money. Many people dislike doing it, seeing it as akin to begging. Others don't do it very well. My view is that everything from governance to specific services is shaped by the need for a sustainable revenue model. You must have the right trustees and other solicitors to make this happen. An organization often does noncore things to raise money to support the essence of an enterprise. That is why the first chapter is on governance. The assembly of askers and connectors in the right numbers and with the right abilities on the board, in the volunteer community, and in senior management, is key. The second chapter is the companion to Chapter 1—namely, the senior management and senior board membership must be revenue/philanthropic oriented to their very core. A church minister, a museum head, a school head, all must be able to create the excitement and ambiance that brings the organization alive and makes people want to contribute financial resources to it. Revenues come in two kinds. The first are fees that can be charged for services or products. Vital to the operation of these organizations, they are not normally sufficient to keep them alive. Rather, there are five major sources of additional revenue that collectively must make up the gap. The first is the annual fund. An annual fund can range from covering 90% of the organization's budget and expenses (a church) to 3% of the budgeted expenses for a large teaching hospital. The second is a capital campaign, targeted at raising money for long-term strategic purposes, which can range from short and modest to large and long. Often a capital campaign provides institutionally transforming gifts. The third source of revenue is planned gifts. Realizable in full on the death of the donor, they often take several decades to materialize. They lay the foundation for infrastructure improvements, financial aid, new programs, and so forth. This is money that you will not get today but will irrevocably get eventually. Fourth are grants secured from foundations. These grants help enable a whole variety of useful projects. Finally, there are galas and all sorts of special fundraising events. These are occasions where people convene to have a good time and also raise funds. University reunions, golf tournaments, and museum black-tie galas are prototypes of these sorts of events.

This book is not devoted to the romance of mission definition and how to shape it. Rather, it is devoted to helping raise the financial resources for these good deeds. It is inelegant and absolutely vital. It puts the burden of social enterprise success on the right shoulders—yours! As a trustee, as a donor, as a connector, or a friend, you are the person most responsible for the success of the social enterprise.

Acknowledgments

THE MATERIAL IN this book is the outgrowth of field research done over the past two decades at Harvard Business School (HBS), and over 40 years of active social enterprise board service by the author. I am particularly grateful to Dean John McArthur at HBS who inspired me to launch this work. His work at Brigham and Women's Hospital as board chair legitimized this type of work for a generation of HBS faculty. I am also grateful to HBS Deans Kim Clark, Jay Light, and Nitin Nohria who have supported my work in this area over a number of years. I am indebted to all the board members and nonprofit executives I have worked with over the years.

All the examples in the book come from real organizations. They are the results of observations of strategic decisions and actions. Some organizations I am able to publicly thank such as Trinity College, Mount Auburn Hospital, and the Dana Hall School. Others must remain anonymous. A special thanks is due to Professors Kasturi "Kash" Rangan and Herman "Dutch" Leonard, the co-heads of HBS's Social Enterprise Initiative for the past decade, who supported my work enthusiastically. I am also grateful to Eliot Snider, a long-term member of Harvard Business School's Social Enterprise

Advisory Board, who particularly focused my attention on philanthropy and how to stimulate it. A special note of thanks goes to my spouse, who supported me through thousands of hours of board meetings; my colleagues Professors Jim Austin, Michael Chu, Mitch Weiss, Allen Grossman, and Alnoor Ebrahim who have been very supportive as has been Matt Segneri and Laura Moon, the last two directors of HBS's Social Enterprise Initiative.

The final responsibility for what appears in this book, of course, is mine. I would also particularly want to thank my administrative assistant Maureen Donovan for the past 40 years for all her valuable administrative support of this work.

1

Asking for Money

OVERWHELMINGLY, WHEN ONE is asked to join the board of a social enterprise, the reaction is one of pleasure and personal pride even if one's other commitments do not allow one to accept. The opportunity to contribute time, energy, and money to an important community or civic enterprise is seen as exciting. Your sense of self-worth is validated by the invitation. Very often, however, one's second comment to the invitation runs along the lines of "I don't have to ask people for money, do I?" Asking for money somehow seems demeaning and distasteful to many individuals. Also the idea of being rejected by a prospective donor is often very personally threatening to one's self-esteem. Even high-powered, otherwise highly self-confident people can turn to jelly when having to ask people for money. A global banker who has put together deals all around the world, described to the author visibly breaking into a cold sweat when forced to solicit other CEOs for seven-figure gifts for charities of mutual interest. He was not used to being a supplicant and did not like it. In his new autobiography *What It Takes*,[1] Steve Schwarzman, chairman of Blackstone and a billionaire, describes how hard it was for him to first raise funds for Blackstone, and then for the Schwarzman

---

[1]Stephen A. Schwarzman, *What It Takes: Lessons in the Pursuit of Excellence* (Simon & Schuster, 2019).

Scholars Program at Tsinghua University in China as he faced rejection after rejection on cold-call solicitations. From top to bottom, there is a common drumbeat of distaste for personal fundraising, which is one of many reasons why professional fundraisers are so well compensated. Yet, without it, otherwise successful organizations can wither and die. In other cases, it is vital to the organization's growth and impact.

Three Propositions

This book is based on three propositions. The first is that most people do not like asking other people for money. (There are fortunately exceptions that are real treasures.) They feel solicitation somehow transforms them into beggars, which they find demeaning. They also worry about being seen as abusing relationships as well as being subjected to requests from the prospective donors for future requests to support their charities. The second proposition is that the most effective advocates for an institution are its supporters. Accordingly, every trustee must give according to their means and in so doing be motivated to fully internalize the mission of the organization and become passionate about it. An inner passion and commitment to its mission, appropriately harnessed, transforms them into very powerful sales agents. They have already voted with their time and treasure, giving instant credibility to the listener to their pitch. Often, the most powerful part of a donor ask presentation is the moment when the solicitor describes how and why they have personally supported the organization. Third, there are things that can be done to relatively easily transform someone from being reluctant to making the ask into someone who, as a sales advocate, can effectively and enthusiastically make an ask. Over time, they can move from easy things, like hosting events to making annual fund asks, capital campaign asks, or even becoming a campaign chair. We simply have to change their mindset for this task.

Different Organizations and Their Needs

Solicitation is of enormous importance to most social enterprises regardless of size and type. The parish church or temple, for example, lives almost completely on members' donations. It is not unusual for 90% of all funds for the year to come from an annual stewardship campaign. Additionally, the funds for special projects for the church, like an elevator acquisition or rebuilding of a bell tower, come from capital campaigns rooted in members' philanthropy. Members must ask other members to make this happen.

In a different vein are schools and universities that have operational cash flow streams such as student tuition, sports contest admission fees, art museum and theatre admission fees, and so forth. These streams are normally inadequate to cover all operating expenses. Large schools and universities (like Exeter and Harvard, for example), therefore, often have large endowments (the result of philanthropy of previous generations) plus large development departments to raise current funds. Endowment income plus annual gifts are how these institutional budgets are balanced. Additionally, these institutions have very active planned-giving programs, which extend the reach of the institution plus periodic multibillion-dollar capital campaigns. Survival of the institution often depends on growing these sources of funds. Alumni and trustees, of course, are critical to the effective making of asks bolstered by both the institution leadership and their development professionals. The lay solicitors who believe deeply in the organization's mission, however, add a special credibility to the fundraising effort.

Similarly, institutions like Boston's Museum of Fine Arts have both annual fund campaigns and capital campaigns. In addition, however, they also have potential donors of individual pieces or collections of art who must be courted. Someone who has given objects to a museum has a credibility that few administrators can have. A final example, nonprofit hospitals depend on capital campaigns for new facilities and research funds. Grateful patients make very useful trustees and are invaluable for making the ask.

Some social enterprises are prosperous, like well-endowed schools, whereas others, like small house museums, already cash strapped, are currently seeing philanthropy dropping at a 7% rate per year because of the difficulty in developing a persuasive sales pitch in this new charitable unfriendly tax world. For some institutions, this funding shortfall is so severe that it means bankruptcy or forced merger. For example, all across New England, small colleges and museums have been closing or merging over the past decade, driven by cash flow shortfalls both in the face of new tax laws and being out of favor with the donors as a charity of choice.

The same consolidation has been going on in the nonprofit hospital sector for the past 30 years. Overlay a map of the hospitals in New England 30 years ago on a map of today's hospitals and one sees a war zone with massive casualties and few survivors. Philanthropic success can literally ensure survival in one's current form or be a key to major transformation or strategic alliance. The ask, in short, is a vital function, and people must be willing to be trained to do it. A social enterprise board needs many skills to exercise its responsibilities effectively. Fundraising skills of its members as givers, connectors, and askers, however, often are critical ones. Consequently, the timeworn phrase GGG (give, get, or get off) is still operative for the board members of many social enterprises. Both givers and connecters at the very top of an organization are essential to the health and survival of many social enterprises. The author was recently accused wryly of being a shameless proponent and advocate of stewardship at the top. It is a sin he will readily confess to.

How to Get Started

How to get started as a new trustee or solicitor in your philanthropic activities? The first thing a new social enterprise trustee or solicitor who is beginning on the path of philanthropic engagement must do is to take the time to truly internalize the mission of the organization in all its nuances. Until you can accurately and passionately describe its mission, you cannot sell it. In my previous book, *Joining a Nonprofit Board: What You Need to Know*,[2] the entire book was devoted to mission and the boards' role in developing and executing it. The second thing that the trustee and donor must do commensurate with one's personal resources is to aggressively support the organization (translation: write a personal check large enough that it hurts). Nothing gives you more credibility in selling an organization's mission and needs to future donors than the fact that you are personally supporting it in a meaningful way. When you are talking about your gift and how you thought about it, you add a priceless note of authenticity to your pitch. A neighbor of the author, when taking over her church's annual stewardship campaign, looked carefully at her previous years' donations and made a stretch gift from her perspective. In the ensuing months, the making of this gift gave an underlying passion to her presentations (both public and one-on-one) which rang with the authenticity of the true believer. This passion was critical to the campaign's ultimate success. Enthusiasm and passion are vital tools in the fundraising tool kit. A good fundraiser has many of the attributes of an evangelist.

A recent leader of a hospital's capital campaign shows the importance of donor longitudinal engagement. Twenty years ago, the individual had been chair of the hospital's board. After serving his term and making a significant seven-digit-figure gift to the hospital's first capital campaign, he had remained involved with the hospital as a corporator and then as its liaison to another medical organization. He also continued being a patient of the hospital, using many of its doctors over the years. As a fundraiser, the 20-plus years of experience and involvement with the hospital underscored

---

[2]F. Warren McFarlan and Marc J. Epstein, *Joining a Nonprofit Board: What You Need to Know* (John Wiley & Sons, 2011), p. 1, Preface.

his deep commitment, which came through in the various solicitation calls and visits he made for the current campaign (including his self-solicitation) to which, as a campaign co-chair, he had first pledged generously.

What the preceding example shows is that a trustee's fundraising skills can be valuable to an organization long after the trustee's term has expired. Former trustees properly engaged are real assets as solicitors in campaigns ranging from those of bricks and mortar to planned giving. Preparation for this role begins when one first becomes engaged as a solicitor and is then successively nurtured and deepened over the years of one's service in many ways. When you recruit trustees, you are engaging their services for the organization not just for their terms as a trustee but also for a very long period of time during which the individual will pass through many roles with the organization beyond that of trustee. Their historical memory of past donors and prior campaign issues, plus their deep commitment, provides invaluable context for today's and tomorrow's campaigns.

Practice makes perfect. The more times someone asks for money, the better they get at it. Additionally, of course, asking a person for support with whom you have developed trust over time yields especially good results. Consequently, matching the right solicitor to the right potential donor is key. Finding matches where mutual respect, common interests, and common history already exist is a good way to get started. Of course, brainstorming with the organization's officers and staff combined with good research in advance of a visit helps in getting an initial dialogue started. A shared hobby, children's common college, a common sport interest, and so forth are all things used to get the conversational ball rolling. As rapport is established, the conversation then naturally moves to the issue at hand. Multiple visits over many years are sometimes required to secure a major pledge. In one case the author is familiar with, it required 50 visits over a decade to secure a $50 million gift. The CEO made so many calls to the donor and other donors in the city where the donor was located that the CEO finally got an apartment there to cut down on travel/living costs. In this context, it should be noted that continuity in connecting potential donors to their previous solicitors can really help. This is also why turnover in an organization's major gift officers can cause real problems as important history and relationships can be lost.

Making the Ask

One of the hardest questions to address is do you ask a prospective donor for a specific dollar number and if so, how high should that number be? (For the record, professional fundraisers say you should always do so.) Several things I have learned that may be helpful:

1. It is almost impossible to insult someone by asking too much. At the worst, they will be flattered to be thought of as being much wealthier than they are.
2. If you ask too low, you may leave a lot of money on the table. The donor may be delighted to get out with such a small commitment given their prior expectations.
3. Inexperienced solicitors tend to blink at the last moment and ask for dramatically less than they were instructed. Sending a team of two (expensive in terms of time) is one way to deal with this, since it is very unlikely the two will collude to lower the ask.
4. Even worse, people will say they asked for more than they did. (Surprise! They sometimes lie.)
5. Approaching someone with the right mindset is key. You are not begging but, rather, offering an unusual and attractive opportunity to the prospective donors to invest in their passion and to have their names associated with it long term. You are not asking for money per se. You are giving a unique opportunity for individuals to contribute to something of importance to them, an opportunity they would not otherwise have. They can make a difference.

6. Start your work as an asker with a known easy prospect on a straightforward project. It will be a confidence builder for you. Building on this success, you can then evolve to more complex donors and projects as you refine your pitch and develop more confidence.

7. For major solicitations, you should prepare a detailed call report shortly after the visit. Prospective donors have quirks and preferences that are really important for askers to understand for effective solicitations in the future. These preferences can in some cases last over decades. The report jogs your memory for your next visit or helps someone else pick up the solicitation thread. Two relationships for an educational institution that evolved over a 40-year period illustrate this point. In each case, what the donor had requested at the time of the initial gift in terms of the types of solicitation processes that the donor would be receptive to was adhered to for many years. However, time and circumstances ultimately changed the preferences of both the donors dramatically. Previously unthinkable projects became desirable alternatives in the fullness of time. "No" sometimes means just "no for now." Careful listening and sensitive longitudinal stewardship are key for successful long-term philanthropy.

8. Don't wait too long to start your visits. Psychological hurdles can build up in your mind, and they get ever larger the longer you worry about them. Get started and let your technique improve through practice. The longer you wait, the bigger the hurdles will seem in your mind until they become insurmountable and you never get started.

9. Develop a short customized pitch in advance of your first meeting with a donor. Donor attention span, particularly at the beginning of a meeting, can be limited. You need to build interest and get the hook in quickly. When you have their attention and rapport has been established, you can then get into the meat and the details.

For the most part, the primary readers of this book are what I call prospective community-level philanthropists. This covers everything from the neighborhood music school to the local community hospital. The recommendations become more complex with a trustee being more of a connector as one deals with mega institutions and mega donors. Harvard's and the Metropolitan Museum's seven-digit-or-more gifts, tend to be handled by the CEO and professional development staff. These organizations have large staffs of major gifts officers, sophisticated databases, and computer software. The role of a donor trustee is more complicated and nuanced in these situations, because the donor calls are often done by a combined trustee/donor and a professional working as a team.

The fundamentals of fundraising, however, are remarkably similar regardless of the size of the organization and the asks. The author recalls interviewing the CEO of an organization that had just completed a successful $1.4 billion capital campaign. The CEO confessed he had gotten his fundraising skills 25 years earlier as a trustee of a local day school where his children went. He found the $25,000 ask for that organization was identical in terms of planning and approach to what he was doing 25 years later as he approached $25 million gift asks.

Your Role as a Solicitor

In summary, the most important thing to understand is that as a fundraiser, your job is not that of a beggar, but rather that of an educator of donors and an expander of horizons about how they can personally impact organizations they care about through their philanthropy. You are providing a service to them—a very valuable one. You are opening up new doors and possibilities both for the donors and for the organization. For the donor, you are introducing them to new ways to contribute to society and enabling them to feel better about themselves. You are bringing enrichment and context into their lives. For the organization, you are providing access to new resources that will enable it to enhance its overall impact. Through all of this, you, as a fundraiser, are transforming the donor organizational relationship from a transactional one to a relational one, which hopefully will endure, reshaping itself appropriately over time. When that happens, scope grows, and hitherto unimaginable philanthropic possibilities become possible. Examples of this will be described throughout the book.

Book Organization

The rest of the book is organized as follows. Chapter 2 deals with governance. Everything related to successful philanthropy flows from governance. Good governance begins with acquiring a CEO with the right interest and skill set for the task ahead. It then involves recruiting the right kind of trustees and solicitors for both donation and connector purposes. This sets the framework for the development department including its staffing structure and size. Chapter 3 focuses on the roles, skills, and challenges of the key people associated with leading and shaping development activities. In short, it is the collective effort of the board chair, the CEO, the head of the development committee, and head of the governance committee and so forth, which spells success. The next three chapters deal with the major sources of philanthropic funds. Chapter 4 covers the annual fund and all the activities associated with the regular raising of funds throughout the year, year after year. Chapter 5 focuses on the special issues involved with capital campaigns. Done at irregular intervals, they often last years, because they secure resources for long-term institution building, including endowed positions, buildings, new educational initiatives, and so forth. Every process and approach is different for the annual fund than for the capital campaign except for the often large overlap in the donor space. Chapter 6 deals with planned gifts and the special estate planning tools to assist effective end-of-life giving. A volunteer often introduces the topic of planned giving to a donor in general terms. Specialists, however, usually make the close, because these gifts are complex with numerous technical issues that must be appropriately and individually resolved, depending on the situation. Chapter 6 also deals with the important role played by foundations in meeting development needs. Chapter 7 focuses on the many events run for development purposes and the things that must be done to make sure the climate is right for fundraising. Tastefully appropriate in tone and well-choreographed events are essential to creating the right climate for effective fundraising. Chapter 8 covers the information system's revolution and how every aspect of development except for the ask has been transformed by the combination of low-cost, large-bandwidth networks, handheld devices like the iPad and iPhone, social media platforms like Facebook, Twitter, and so on. Chapter 9 focuses on the special challenges that the micro social enterprise (revenues below $1 million and often no paid staff) faces. Hundreds of thousands of these base of the social enterprise organizations exist across the country. They are important and face unique challenges. Finally, Chapter 10 focuses on how an individual can improve their fundraising skills. It is the author's contention that with proper training, it is easy for you to become good in this arena and your newly acquired skills will give you great satisfaction.

Two roles will repeatedly surface in the book—namely, that of the solicitor and that of the connector. Exhibits 1.1 and 1.2 highlight some of the characteristics that the best of these individuals contain. A question for you as you read this book is which one best describes you and how can you improve your skills.

Exhibit 1.1: The Solicitor

1. Understands the organization's issues and needs
2. Has made the pledge
3. Has internalized a three-minute elevator pitch
4. Tries to understand prospective donor's mindset
5. Comes with an evangelist's mindset
6. Builds in listening time
7. Is often a builder of an enduring institutional relationship (each visit is one of a series of contacts)
8. Leaves a written record of call points to shape future calls

Exhibit 1.2: The Connector

- Understands the organization's issues and needs
- Has made the pledge (size irrelevant)
- Knows or has access to many potential donors (individuals and foundations)
- Is willing to share contacts
- Has done substantial solicitation in the past (probably for other organizations)
- Has experience in other development organizations
- Has no obvious current conflicts of interest

2

Governance

ODDLY ENOUGH, THE right place to begin the discussion of fundraising is with the governance committee of the organization's board of trustees (see Figure 2.1). At the core, this group is responsible for assembling and developing the fundraising talent and leadership on the board, and setting the tone for development. These trustees must facilitate the assembly of a core network of givers and connectors, and ensure the right level of staff is present in the organization. In times of a head change, the governance committee works very closely with the search committee to assess how important fundraising skills will be in the next head, and to ensure that the final candidate possesses them. As noted earlier, it is not unusual for 50% or more of a nonprofit CEO's time to be devoted to fundraising activities over their years of leadership (clearly, therefore, this is usually a very relevant skill requirement).

Governance Committee Composition

The governance committee of the board (see Figure 2.1) is normally made up of its most senior trustees. It has six critical roles:

1. Selecting, evaluating, and coaching of the CEO. It often does the selection by commissioning a special search committee of the board for the task.

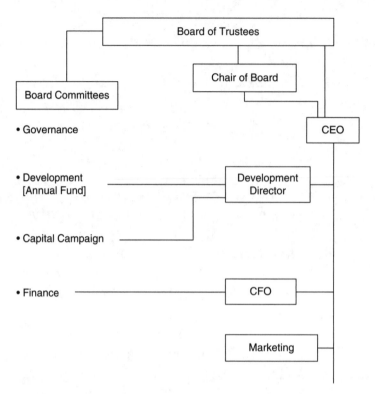

Figure 2.1   Partial Organization Chart

2. Recruiting new members of the board, making sure the skills are on the board for future leadership, and ensuring the various tasks that need to be done can be staffed.
3. Having a deep understanding of the strategy of the organization and what it needs to do for the future.
4. Recruiting the necessary people onto the board who can mobilize appropriate development. This is normally done by adding potential major donors and connectors on the board. This group must be composed of individuals who will not disrupt the other governance activities of the board but who can energize the organization's development activities.

5. Selecting and appointing board officers and committee chairs. In particular, they need to have a multiyear view of potential succession.

6. Determining and enforcing length of board and officer term limits.

A Case Study

A recent case study described here illustrates how governance committee organization played out in one organization. The organization was an over 500 student K - 12 independent school. As the story begins, it had a highly experienced board (averaging over 20 years of service) including a board chair with over 10 years of service. The school in the past decade had added some very capital-intensive program expansions for which the funding had been done through debt, not philanthropy. The organization had a very modest endowment. Its facilities were old. Fundraising had not been a board priority for at least the past decade. For the past decade, most trustee gifts each year had been in the $1,000 range or less. They were not a major source of funds for the school. Neither was the success of the annual fund a priority for them.

The case starts with a new head being picked after the retirement of his predecessor. The new head, after surveying the landscape and his competitive positioning, launched multiple initiatives. The first was rebuilding a development department to energize its annual fund and create an alumni and friends database. School publications were modernized. New parent trustees were brought onto a board that simultaneously installed term limits for both the trustees and officers. A careful study was launched of the state of the physical facilities. Major inadequacies were identified, which appeared to significantly impact the quality of the programs and their marketing appeal.

The previous board was composed of people of stature, but with both relatively limited giving capacity (or at least giving habits) and interest in that domain. In going through its once in every decade external accreditation, the board's and head's attention were drawn by the evaluator's focus on the school's high debt in relation to its competitors, as well as the absence of a significant annual fund, combined with no plans for a capital campaign.

As part of addressing these issues, the board (at the urging of the head) recruited onto it a new trustee, who was very familiar with the need for a school to have access to both capital campaign dollars and annual fund dollars. The new board member was asked to head a newly formed governance committee. Almost immediately identifying capital shortage and aging facilities as key issues, the governance committee then stimulated the recruitment of four new development-oriented trustees to the board, who had a deep commitment to the school because their children were enrolled. They had both significant personal resources, as well as strong links to other individuals in the community who had substantial resources. A building project of great strategic programmatic relevance to the school was brought forward. Almost immediately, funding inside the board jumped to 50% of the project's costs, all fueled by the new and relatively new trustees.

At the same time, an experienced new development director was recruited from outside to energize the development infrastructure both to support fundraising in general and for this project in particular. The new director and the board rapidly mobilized non-board parents to contribute the other 50% of the project over six months, and a transforming project was launched. Five years down the road, millions had been raised from all sources around this project and two subsequent equally transformative projects.

To make this happen, the governance committee nearly doubled the board size with 80% being significant donors and all being donors sparked by the dynamism of the projects, and the transformation that they promised in the school's programs. Importantly, enrollment in the school jumped by 150 new full-paying students who were attracted to the new proposition. The trustees, who sparked the initial effort, rolled off the board (courtesy of term limits) and were replaced by like-minded individuals (mostly parents and grandparents) with similar resources and passion. Structures to attempt to keep former trustees engaged were put in place. Board rebuilding has become a never-ending project (courtesy again of term limits). The key points from this case are:

1. Building a development-oriented culture in an institution takes time. The preceding story took over five years to play out. As noted, attention must continue to be paid to the board's regeneration as each generation of development-oriented trustees reaches the end of their term limits. The new set of trustees must also have the right combination of vision and personal financial resources to continue the transformation.
2. Development-oriented leadership was key to this transformation. In this example, it was a CEO who had no deep development experience but an appetite for growth, who was supported by a total reconstituted board that contained deep development capabilities. The spark for creating this was the member who had both development and governance experience. First came the board reconstitution, along with new development staff leadership, and then a series of transforming projects in rapid succession.
3. The assembly of a much larger board of donors and connectors made a huge difference. At its height, the board grew from 16 to 34. This allowed the mobilization of many donors.

Over the next two years, the board then went back to 24 in the absence of major new projects.

Board Recruiting and Structure

The most important point of this case is that the board itself took responsibility for raising the overall fundraising capabilities of the organization initially prodded by the CEO and the external accrediting organization. It began by reconstructing itself to have dramatically expanded development capabilities. If governance was the only role of a social enterprise board, it would contain six to eight members in total (much like a typical for-profit board). The development focus, however, drives a social enterprise board to be much larger (4–20 additional trustees are the norm for midsize and larger organizations). Supported by a paid development staff, a board often has two development committees; one is a development committee that worries about annual fundraising, donor relations, research, and so on. The second is a capital campaign committee, which may operate as an ad hoc committee over a 5- to 10-year horizon. The development committee normally has overall responsibility for all development activities except for the capital campaign with which it has a tight liaison. The development department includes activities such as the annual fund, planned giving, alumni clubs, stewardship, research, and major gift officers. The development-oriented trustees are normally divided between the development committee and the capital campaign committees as their primary board work. Special events (fundraisers) are also part of this cluster of activities (discussed in Chapter 7). Often younger trustees gravitate to the annual fund activities, whereas the older ones wind up on the capital campaign committee because of their often higher giving potential and deeper links to potential donors.

Term Limits

The governance committee plays a critical role in the selection of potential trustees, their assignments, and their ultimate rotation off the board. It is also responsible for recruiting overseers/corporators (supporters of the organization who convene once or twice a year to give advice). The existence of term limits defined by the governance committee ensures that there will be continued turnover in these boards and officer positions. This turnover is critical in allowing space for new development-oriented trustees to join the board. With regard to term limits, one or two positions on the board may be reserved for people of such unusual skill or development capability that you do not want to lose their link to the organization and, therefore, want to insulate them from the constraint of term limits. Discipline, however, has to be maintained to ensure this insulation does not get out of control. In a recently studied case of an organization with an ironclad term limit of eight years, one trustee is now in his 17th year on the board. The individual has headed two capital campaigns and a building is named for him. A guiding principle about term limits is that you need them but "don't do stupid things." Excessive reliance on standard procedures can sometimes get you into unfortunate decisions that can harm the organization (exceptions, of course, can have their problems as well).

Trustee Career Path

Several years before a trustee retires, efforts must be made to work out their level of engagement with the organization post-trusteeship (above all, you do not want a deeply committed trustee transferring their wealth and philanthropy to a competing organization). Trusteeship should be seen as simply one part of a life-long period of an individual's engagement with the organization. Planning this engagement in advance is critical. A few trustees may go on to be trustees emeritus or emerita (you must be careful, however, not to crowd the board room). Others join special program advisory committees, hopefully in areas of great personal interest. Others may stay on one or two board committees (investment is a frequent one, as is planned giving and capital campaign). Still others may move to special advisory boards called "the corporation" or overseers that meet once or twice a year. Many will turn out to be effective solicitors and connectors for future campaigns.

Efforts are often made to get key corporators involved in advisory boards and programs that require regular contact with the organization's staff. This contact can help facilitate planned giving discussions to extend the impact of the former trustee's philanthropy beyond their life span. For some trustees, however, unfortunately there will not be an ongoing role because of lack of fit between their skills and the organization's interests, interpersonal conflict, and so forth. That is too bad but inevitable.

Building Trustee Engagement

Involving a trustee in a project's implementation complexities can get their visceral juices flowing, and in the right circumstances, commitments can flow beyond imagination. The author watched in fascination as a $3 million building project sponsored by a donor ran into local zoning issues. With the donor on the project team (including his involvement in direct negotiation with the city bureaucrats), over six years the project budget ultimately grew to over $20 million, much of it covered by the original donor who was appalled by the regulatory environment and what he saw as regulatory abuse. Fortunately, he reacted with both fury and also personal generosity. The deeper one gets involved in execution details, the more one's personal financial prudence can fly out the door as commitment to task completion grows at any cost.

Donor Recognition

Donor recognition is a funny topic. Some people want it and consequently every corner of a building can be filled with plaques. Intriguingly, not everyone, however, wants recognition, even for very sizeable gifts. They simply want to do good. The story of a major donor to a university, who served first as a trustee and then as a member of an advisory committee, is illustrative. As his most recent gift, 25 years after his initial trustee service, he gave an eight-digit anonymous gift to cut the cost of endowing staff positions by one-third. This lowered cost enabled otherwise financially stretched individuals to endow staff positions in their name and brought substantial new funds to the organization. The major donor found it appealing that his anonymous gift to a major project encouraged other people to make gifts. In other venues, he wanted some recognition so people knew he supported a project, but almost always it was recognition at levels well below his actual gift.

Multigenerational Trustees

The work of donor management by the governance committee can be multigenerational. Consider the following story. A university alum had great success professionally in the for-profit world. He then followed this work up by leading a nonprofit institution with distinction for a decade. On his retirement, his alma mater gave him a picture of their campus as part of thanking him as an alum for giving such distinguished service to society. To their surprise, several weeks later, he appeared on campus to present a $20 million gift for a vital new facility. In subsequent years, he became a trustee of the institution and ultimately head of its next capital campaign, where his philanthropy only grew. Today his children (also alums) are now trustees and supporters.

Summary

Relationships grow in complex and unexpected ways over long periods of time. In ways not always recognized in the literature, governance and development are absolutely interlinked. The cold reality is that the closer people are to the heart of an organization, the more generous some of them become. It should not matter, but the fact is, it does. Unfortunately, the larger a deliberative group is, the longer and more diffuse its discussions can become. This means garrulous donor trustees are a real burden versus those who drop off for a short nap (as long as they do not snore!). This puts a special burden on the governance committee to properly vet potential board candidates to make sure they will comfortably fit into the board activities. When there is doubt, a year's advance service on a board committee can provide useful insights.

In summary, the governance committee of the board is fundamentally responsible for spearheading the creation of a board and network of supporters, who can mobilize the resources to allow the organization's mission to become reality. This task can take years to execute. Exhibit 2.1 identifies key levers that can be activated by a governance committee to impact the development environment in an organization. The organization needs not only board members who can help bring the mission to reality, but also a CEO and board chair who share this perspective and have the skills to make it happen. Juggling this among other priorities of the organization is very hard for the governance committee. It can be particularly hard to get started, in cases where it is hard to find mission supporters, let alone affluent ones. From this perspective, geographically centralized communities, such as churches, schools, and universities, can find it much easier to attract donors than cause-oriented programs such as healthcare in homeless shelters.

Exhibit 2.1: Governance—Levers That Can Be Activated

- Size of board
- Number of development trustees on board
- Trustee postboard service links
- Number and length of terms for a trustee
- Head of development committee serves on governance committee
- Vice-chair exception—a great way to keep indispensable trustees who have completed their term
- Friends and potential trustees serve on board committee

Questions a trustee should ask about governance

- Has the board taken into account the development needs of the organization in building its board and officers? Is there an appropriate development climate in the boardroom?
- Is the governance committee appropriately focused on development as it recruits new members and officers?
- Are appropriate mechanisms in place to ensure lifelong connectedness of key trustees as their terms expire?
- Have we found ways to engage friends of the organization in advisory committees to keep them close, even if they are not board candidates?
- Capital campaign committees and annual fund committees chaired by trustees and composed of friends are widely used tools to broaden development involvement. Are they being used in your organization?

3

The Players

DEVELOPMENT IS LIKE a minuet. There are a lot of specific processes you need to go through. How you staff and execute them, however, is highly idiosyncratic. It depends on your size, the nature of your giving base, and your culture, among other things. There are a number of people who play critical policy roles in shaping development. These include the chairman of the board, head of the governance committee, head of the board's development committee, head of the board's capital campaign committee (only at capital campaign time), the organization's CEO, and the development head. Each of these individuals has a key responsibility in ensuring the success of the organization's development activities regardless of whether one is dealing with a neighborhood nursery school on one end of a size spectrum or a top-50 teaching hospital on the other end of the size spectrum. Each person's role will be discussed in detail in the following sections.

The Development Director

This individual is central to the success of the development effort. An effective development director requires extraordinary interpersonal skills to manage relationships with multiple constituencies, both inside and outside the organization. The director must also be able to handle large amounts of operational details and complexity in an almost flawless way. Such people are hard to find. It is one of the reasons why compensation for these jobs and their turnover rates are so high. Burnout is a constant worry. The following example illustrates the complexity of the job.

A small college decided it needed to dramatically ramp up its annual fund and capital campaign capabilities. The annual fund was getting less than 50% participation by alumni for reunion classes (versus a 90% rate at comparable colleges), and a capital campaign had not been done in living memory. There were significant unfunded programmatic and capital fund needs. To get started, a new development director was recruited at the instigation of the board and head. Everything had to start from scratch as existing internal systems were primitive. The development director spent the first year and a half getting alumni mailing-address lists prepared, identifying potential alumni donors. It also organized each class of alumni to have a development staff member as class fundraiser coordinator. This work was necessary, was well done, and laid a solid foundation for the future, but it was not enough. The new director was good at building processes especially for managing operational detail, but lacked the skills to excite and energize key donors and volunteers. In every encounter with alums and board members, the director came across as a dull bureaucratic unexciting person. Unanimously, the board came to the reluctant conclusion that the individual could not finish what had been launched and get the college to the next level. Ultimately, the director was phased out.

A search process was launched, resulting in the hiring of a highly charismatic number-two development person from a much larger organization as the new development director. This individual had deep face-to-face fundraising experience in his background. Starting with board self-solicitation and joint solicitations of major prospects by the development head and the head of the college, a $14 million project was launched with its fundraising completed within a year (nothing of this sort had been previously done). The development director then dramatically expanded the donor base such that it was able to sustain a second project of equal size. Donor engagement was the director's great skill. Repeatedly, the director and staff spotted major potential donors, introduced them to the CEO, and managed their progression as donors. Unfortunately, although brilliant in starting and managing donor relationships, internal management of a new development staff was challenging. Two years of over 50% turnover slowed part of the effort as the development director, the CEO, and head of the development committee all worked on the issue. Fortunately, the effort was successful, as, over three years, reunion class gifts doubled.

The job of the development director, of course, is much more than just donor management. Planner, manager, donor relationship manager, and builder of internal management processes are just a few of the skills needed to be successful. This is why in most social enterprise organizations, this is the second highest paid job (just below the CEO) and also unfortunately, the highest turnover job. It is hard work. When a new CEO is appointed, often a new development head is quickly recruited to complement the CEO's skills and personality. This turnover can be a big problem since, as noted later, major gift officers and relationship managers really benefit from longitudinal donor relationships often lasting a decade or longer. The responsibilities of the development department head normally include the following.

Managing an Annual Fund

The annual fund group (whether one volunteer or one hundred paid people) must be able to both ask for money personally and mobilize volunteers to do the same. These personal fundraisers communicate with donors in person, by mail, by email, and by direct telephone solicitation. They recruit and train volunteers as well as run telethons. They must be basically extrovert in personality, be able to handle rejection without taking it personally, and have great stamina. Obviously, for the bigger asks, they need to have a deep understanding of the organization's needs and priorities to appropriately guide donor conversations. In small organizations, the majority of this work is done by volunteers rather than by paid annual fund solicitors. For example, a recently completed $1 million church annual stewardship campaign was 100% done by volunteers with the clerical work supported by the church accountant and parish secretary.

Managing Major Gift and Capital Campaign Officers

These individuals need different skills from the annual fund solicitors because they are asking for significantly larger amounts of money over often very long time periods. Furthermore, their asks (which may be multiple) also often take place over an extended period of time. Many individuals give multiple gifts over the years. I ran into a development officer at the airport recently on his way to Hong Kong for his 15th trip in the past decade. It was to be three days of action-packed meetings with old donors, hot prospect new donors, and introductory calls to hopefully eventual donors. This was before Coronavirus Covid-19 and the closing of Hong Kong to all foreign visitors.

A key part of the job in managing major gifts officers is keeping their morale up. Like great baseball players, along with their successes, they also strike out more than half the time. They must be good listeners and outstanding relationship managers. Their job involves managing multiple encounters with individual donors in between donor visits by the CEO (often accompanied by the major gifts officer). There is great development value to maintaining longitudinal donor relationships. Personal comfort with each other and shared history in managing previous gifts can really help.

Managing Research

Research capability is a very important front end of a development organization. Their job is to both identify potential new donors for the institution and spot existing donors whose circumstances and/ or priorities have changed (hopefully in a positive way). They also need to be alert to any whiff of ethical/legal problems with existing or future donors (you don't want to get enmeshed in a Jeffrey Epstein[1] situation). Repeatedly, enthusiasm for closing a major gift from a new donor can blind solicitors to potential reputational risks associated with it. This research can be particularly helpful in providing nuggets for conversation starters by uncovering potential links/shared interests between the donor and the person making the visit. A child in a college that one of yours went to or a shared sports interest are examples of good conversation starters. At his first meeting of a recently joined board, the author was challenged by a board member on a complex issue. He did not know the board member. A Google search, however, revealed a personal linkage in that she was the daughter of a previous business associate whom he had worked with a decade earlier. Two emails later and a meeting together, we had become fast friends and subsequently launched several development initiatives together. Good research can highlight both networks of shared interests and provide insight to one's priorities. The more you know as a solicitor about a prospect, the more effective you can be in baiting the hook. Trout fishing and development have a lot in common.

Supervising Operations

This is an unglamorous but unfortunately very important part of development. It is critical, for example, that an organization

---

[1]A convicted sexual predator who made major gifts to Harvard and MIT over a 20-year period, which were ill-advisedly accepted.

efficiently and accurately record all pledge payments, security transactions, donor change of address, and so forth. One hundred percent
accuracy is the goal. Lost checks, for example, can cause considerable donor angst and even disaffection (every gift needs a personalized note of thanks). Forgetting to put names on donor recognition
lists causes difficulty (even something as small as misspelling names
can be an issue). In this world of cheap ubiquitous data processing,
there are both opportunities and risks for almost every organization
(see Chapter 8 for more details). Even the smallest organizations
now make significant use of data processing. In a recent stewardship
campaign for a church, one evening the campaign chair wanted to
know how they were doing with previous years' donors ranked by
size of gift to specifically identify those who had not yet given. Five
minutes later, he was handed a list of 71 donors of the previous
year, ranked by size of gift, who had not yet pledged this year. Ten
minutes later, the 10 largest laggards had been assigned to individuals for immediate corrective action including email, telephone, and
snail mail (all implemented within 48 hours with great success).
Accurate accessible data really matters.

A Google search of the names revealed that one of the laggard
large donors had recently lost their job. Solicitation was canceled
for the individual and substituted with a pastoral call to express
empathy and support. In the electronic world of 2020, orders of
magnitude more data can be at the researcher's fingertips than was
true a decade earlier (we will skip over the thorny field of data privacy for the moment). As a result, you can be much more informed,
sensitive, and nuanced in your solicitation approach.

You must be careful to fully understand the technology's impact
on your task. You can make a big mistake by not analyzing carefully the full impact of what you are doing. For example, in this
new world of electronic information access and the Internet, some
organizations began to go to just online reporting of donor giving
to reduce donor report printing costs. Be careful! Just because you
can do it doesn't mean you should do it. It turns out that there are

hidden behavioral consequences of making this change, which can have unfortunate real-world impact on giving. A college or school donor annual report lying on a desk or coffee table is often browsed through by prospective donors sitting in front of a TV or just passing time, months after it is sent out. Questions that are asked as they scan the material include who else in the class gave? What about members of the classes above or below you? Did your children give? What about relatives and friends? This data can change one's mind about personal philanthropy. This type of ad hoc information scanning is almost impossible to do if one is using an iPad or PC to access the donor report.

Not long ago, the author was browsing the annual donor report of a school where he was a corporator. After checking that his contribution had been recorded correctly, he went to the section of the report on his daughter's class contributions. He was pleased to see she had pledged at a certain level for the past decade and was continuing to do so. He also noted two of her classmates whose fathers he knew had also given (making it easy to strike up a conversation with one of the fathers the next week during a chance encounter). All that transferred into warm feelings for the school, which influenced the following year's pledge by the author. These documents are not just reporting documents, but rather marketing documents to help stimulate additional giving by both past donors and new ones. They are marketing documents particularly for older donors and major donors. Some organizations that went to full online reporting for efficiency reasons are now reversing course for these marketing reasons.

Quality control of communications is very important. Misspelling of names can undo the intimacy and sense of connectedness that one is trying to create. Changes of email addresses and mailing addresses are unglamorous activities that have to be continually attended to. In short, the soft underbelly of development is operations. It must be carefully staffed to ensure it is an asset and not a liability to the overall development activity.

Stewardship

This is sometimes handled by major-gift officers and sometimes by a special group. Effectively done, it is not just reporting to past donors how their gifts are being utilized, but rather a marketing tool to encourage future gifts. Each stewardship contact reminds the donor of their gift and how it is being currently used. Letters from recipients of scholarships, research grants or travel grants, as well as reports to how donated funds are being utilized can inspire the donors to expand their commitments and also encourage others to make similar gifts. Distribution of an annual stewardship report is a very good time for a major gifts officer to call on the donor to review the gift's impact and brainstorm about future gifts. Donor cultivation through effective stewardship is one of the most important tools of development. Often, too much attention is paid to finding new donors and not enough attention is paid to expanding the commitment and engagement of existing donors.

Good development at the core is characterized by the word *relational*, not the word *transactional*, with stewardship being vital. Individuals are often completely unaware of what they can do once they have made the decision to become engaged with an organization. Good stewardship can really help in this regard over long time periods. As noted earlier, for major donors, active continuous engagement with both major donors and past trustees is critical so they do not get picked off by development departments of other competing social enterprise organizations.

In the course of a recent hospital capital campaign for a new emergency room, a donor from a previous campaign was being briefed on how their $5 million gift to the campaign seven years earlier was being utilized. After this update was done, the development director then gave a five-minute outline on the new campaign's objectives, which were very different in impact from the previous ones. This elicited the response from the donor that he would like to hear more. Jumping to the end of the story, five months later, after the initial donor stewardship presentation, the donor said they would like to pledge $2.5 million to the new project. Additionally, if the hospital could find another $2.5 million donor, the donor would match it with another $2.5 million. It is the author's judgment that because of the first $2.5 million pledge, the likelihood of finding a second one has gone up sharply. Gifts of that size to this organization for this campaign have now been legitimized. It is always exciting to find new donors. Often, however, great value comes from managing and harvesting old relationships. Stewardship is not an overhead item but an offensive weapon.

Sourcing Matching Gifts

A decade ago in a Diocesan capital campaign, a long-time supporter of the diocese, when solicited for $1 million, said he was tired of always being the sole lead donor. He would be happy to pledge $1 million if two other people could be found to give $1 million each. His ground rule was that this had to be money from new donors who had never given to the Diocese at this level before. Six months later with their attention sharpened, the development staff and their consultants located two additional gifts. When the first stake is planted in the ground on a high-end gift, it becomes the new normal and it becomes easier to identify other gifts at that level. The development director, the CEO, and the head of the development committee all collaborated to make this happen.

Establishing Giving Societies

These are important tools to help ratchet annual giving, particularly for new donors. Each year, members of the development staff try to advance a donor to the next level as both the donor's resources grow and their affection for the organization grows. Some donors move their gift up for pure recognition and vanity reasons (perfectly fine). Other donors get seduced to an ever-higher level of engagement with the organization as their commitment to its mission grows, and they pay no attention to what giving society they are in.

Creating Corporation/Overseer Support

Giving societies morph at the high end into formal advisory groups. An advisory group mechanism that is often used in larger organizations is the corporation or overseers group mentioned earlier. This group of supporters of an organization meets once or twice a year to be briefed on key issues facing the organization and give advice on how these issues might be addressed (the meeting should be no more than one-quarter briefing and at least three-quarters advice giving). People love to talk and are much less enthusiastic about listening, particularly to formal briefings. Speaking also often sharpens one's interest as one is forced to organize their thoughts more carefully. This group is normally composed of future trustees, past trustees, and friends of the organization for whom, for one reason or another, trusteeship was not appropriate (usually time constraints or conflicts of interest). This group may run to well over 100 people. They tend to be elected for terms of two or three years with no limit on the number of terms an individual can serve (as long as the individual remains an active supporter of the organization). For example, a major museum struggling to prepare for a capital campaign recently created a corporation that grew from zero to 40 people over a three-year period. All these were individuals with significant giving potential and interest in some aspect of the museum. Beyond their corporation role, these individuals can be a nucleus of a capital campaign. It, of course, takes staff time to plan and deliver events for this group.

The corporation/overseers represent reserve giving potential. A school, several years ago, was working to top off a $55 million capital campaign. Three-quarters of the way to the goal, they went to their corporators, a group of 150 people. To be a corporator, one gave a minimum of $2,500 year. The corporators on a one-time basis were asked to give $10,000 to the campaign. Over 100 responded and $2 million was raised. The corporation is also an important mechanism to bind people to an organization for future campaigns and not let them wander off. It is another step to life-long connectedness and a bridge to planned giving (Chapter 6).

Advisory Committees

An important development challenge (noted earlier) is capturing former trustees after their term ends and before they deploy elsewhere after their period of service. For larger organizations, a series of advisory committees, which meet once a year around particular focus areas inside the organization, is a frequently used mechanism for binding people to you long term. Harvard University, for example, has dozens of these "ad hoc advisory committees" ranging from ones for academic schools like the Business School or Medical School, to service areas like the Library, Art Museum, information technology, or activities like the athletic department or friends of a particular sport. Where there are potential donors, there are usually advisory committees. For museums, there are committees for specific collections or for galleries. For hospitals, specific research/ education initiative committees are created.

These committees are particularly important for engaging older donors as their focus evolves from annual fund and capital campaign into planned giving and bequests. Larger organizations frequently have planned giving staff that focus just on the vehicles appropriate for senior givers. For example, before one's 50th reunion at Harvard College, you never hear about charitable annuities and charitable remainder trusts. Conversely, at one's 60th and 65th reunions, that is practically all that the development department is staffed up to talk about (see Chapter 6). Societies are often formed to visibly honor those who have included the social enterprises in their will or estate plan.

Appropriately Distributing and Coordinating Development Staff

In large decentralized organizations like universities and hospitals, there is intense pressure to decentralize development staff close to operating units, which have their specific unique needs. Enormous tension often exists between a centralized development group, which may be driving specific institutional priorities as opposed to the more narrow ones of the decentralized development units. The problem is if a donor is a graduate of a local unit, she may want no part of a set of central university priorities. Similarly, the cardiac patient of a hospital may want to give to just the cardiac program at the hospital. In either case, if a proposed gift is shaped and driven by the central development group, the mismatch between what they want and the donor desires may be such that the donor may wind up giving nothing to the organization.

These are real issues. Interestingly, however, the shape often evolves over time for specific individuals. Some years ago, for example, a faculty member was in charge of local development at a graduate school that was part of a university that also had a centralized development function. He had just completed a very successful solicitation of an alum of the graduate school for a multimillion-dollar gift. As the meeting wrapped up, the alum turned to the graduate school faculty member and asked for a personal favor. The alum said he was deeply involved with his undergraduate college and felt harassed by the continual attempts by the rest of the university (whose graduate school he had attended) to solicit him for money when the only part of the university the alum was interested in was the graduate school of which he was an alum. The alum was deeply committed to supporting his undergraduate college and had no interest in the undergraduate college of the university where he went to graduate school. The graduate school faculty member then took steps to ensure that the rest of the university's development activities would stay away from this alum. The alum was very grateful and continued to loyally support the graduate school.

However, a decade later, one of the alum's children was both admitted and subsequently went to the undergraduate part of the university. At this stage, of course, the faculty member of the graduate school told the alum that the embargo had been lifted and the alum in his new role as a parent of an undergraduate student at the university was now fair game for solicitation by the rest of the university. The very happy alum ultimately wound up supporting both parts of the university.

Finally, it must be stressed that both annual fund and major gifts activities have to be carefully planned and organized to be successful. Past donor history must be combined with current data to spot emerging pockets of weaknesses. LYBNT (last year, but not this year) data needs careful analysis for potential weaknesses and areas for extra focus. Each type of organization does these tasks differently. Schools, for example, do much of their fundraising by class (parents of those classes enrolled in the school and alumni classes for graduates). Colleges do it heavily by class of alumni (parent giving is not so important). Museums do it by town/region and by type of collections, whereas hospitals do it by geography and by disease type. Designing the initial wave of donor contacts and who and how to follow up these contacts is key and must be customized to the organization. Disciplined follow-up of nonrespondents is key. Personal calls on the individual are best with telephone calls, voice mail, email, and letters, preferential in descending order. Development committee members (discussed below) are normally significant donors or connectors and persuaders extraordinaire.

In summary, development organization structure reflects the type of sources of financial support received by the organization. This, of course, also means very different development director skills and personalities being needed for different organizations.

Head of Development Committee

The development committee of the board is the group of trustees responsible for raising philanthropic funds for the organization. As such, in conjunction with the CEO, they oversee the development director and his/her department. This committee head's job can be very time consuming. It is so intense and time consuming that after two to three years, many heads of the committee burn out. Among the key attributes the committee head must have are the following.

Great Interpersonal and Listening Skills

The head of the development committee must have a good relationship with the head of the organization. There must be a clear mutual understanding between them of the organization's priorities. The development committee head needs a good feel of the nuances of the skill sets of the head and what a productive set of requests for her time on development activities should be. Some heads do better in one-on-one discussions, others in small groups, while still others sparkle in large group settings. While one is good in one setting, often the individual is not so good in other settings. This reality is critical to understand in planning how to most effectively use the CEO's limited time resource.

Highly Persuasive but Sensitive

The development committee chair must have a knack for being able to attract donors and connectors to the committee and get them to commit to doing personal soliciting or networking. The job is not dissimilar to being a cheerleader. A highly persuasive and positive view of life is absolutely essential. Shadows of doubt must be well concealed. Needless to say, the head of the committee should be a good connector and solicitor in their own right.

Persistence

Persistence is a critical virtue for the head of the development committee and its members. The best way to be a successful solicitor is keep coming back and, in a tasteful way, wear potential donors down by educating them. As the size of the individual donor contribution grows, a better job must be done to match the right solicitor with the right donor. For example, in a recent church campaign the top seventh of LYBNTs were assigned to the senior development trustee, who brought them all in at or above the previous years' levels. The bottom seventh of the LYBNT's mostly younger donors were assigned to a young new trustee who did a tremendous job bringing them in. Having proven his skill next year he will be assigned a group of more affluent LYBNT's donors (in the spirit that no good deed should go unpunished).

Fearlessness

The best development committee heads solicit with conviction (having internalized the mission and made their gift). They put away ghosts of potential rejection. Not only that, but also more importantly, they motivate others to do the same. A positive attitude coupled with several recognized personal soliciting successes can do wonders in inspiring a team. In a recent $1.0 million annual campaign, two unexpected pledge-doubling gifts sourced by the development committee head got the conversation going that the aggressive campaign goal could actually be achieved. Talked about successes can eventually become much bigger in moving human behavior than the actual success itself. By building the aurora of invincibility you, in fact, become invincible. Myths are important.

Comfortable in a Networked Environment

The reality is that there is great ambiguity in development relationships with a lot of blurry management structures. For example, the development head is not just responsible to the head of the organization, but also to the head of the development committee. A recent case shows how complex this can be.

The head of the organization and the head of the board development committee decided jointly to hire a new head of development. Because the proposed hire was controversial, the board chair was also consulted. All agreed the upside benefit of the hire offset the downside risk. The new hire was made.

Unfortunately, the new hire did not work out. He was unable to develop good relationships with the organization head, who found him disruptive. The development committee head was concerned because the new hire was not only failing to bring in significant new gifts but was having trouble relating to the traditional donors. After eight months, the organization head finally decided the development head was not going to work out and the development head was let go. Unfortunately, the development committee head's opinion was not asked for. He only learned about the severance after the individual was let go. Having put a lot of his time into trying to make the relationship work, only to have the rug pulled out from him with no consultation by the CEO, the development committee head became disaffected with the organization and quietly resigned first as committee head, and then from the board. With that, a mid-six-figure capital gift prospect (the development committee chair) was off the table (very significant to the organization). The board chair was not able to intervene in time. The loser in all of this was the organization, which lost a potential major financial donor and was left with no head of development. All this simply illustrates how complex development can be.

The CEO

The final judgment on the performance of a development director is ultimately that of the CEO (previous example). She may (and should) get advice on the matter, but it is ultimately her decision.

As noted earlier, it must be recognized that up to 50% or more of the CEO's time is spent on the donor relations aspect of development. The donors overwhelmingly make their gifts in anticipation that the CEO will see that the hoped-for benefits of the gift are ultimately achieved. Consequently, when a CEO is fired or quits, usually the flow of philanthropy to the organization dramatically drops and stays at that low level until a new CEO is picked and has time to make her mark. When Larry Summers unexpectedly stepped down at Harvard, the university was just two months away from public announcement of a multibillion-dollar capital campaign. Immediately everything was frozen. It was three years later before it could be picked up under a new CEO and development leadership. In these situations, development people often want to push ahead, but it is usually a bad idea.

It goes without saying that the CEO must have confidence in her development officer. The reality is the CEO will spend more time with her development officer than with anyone else in the organization. It is one reason as noted earlier that so many new CEOs bring a new development officer into the organization shortly after they take the job.

Donor relationships take a long time to emerge and solidify. For this reason, a capital campaign often takes place at the back end of an administration to harvest all the donor/CEO relationships that have developed over the years that the CEO has led the organization. For example, the capital campaign for a church diocese was started some years ago when the presiding bishop (who had served 14 years) was 65 (retirement age was 70). Five years later at the time of his retirement, a $30 million capital campaign built heavily around his personal relationships with parishioners and ministers of churches in the diocese had been successfully completed.

A CEO must be relatively sure of the success of a capital campaign plan before committing his organization and his career to it. Not every organization is ready. A dispassionate feasibility study is standard practice. Several years ago, a house museum was anxious to launch a campaign both to address building maintenance and endowment. A consulting firm was retained to do the feasibility study for this project. Unfortunately, the firm came back with the clear conclusion that the museum's brand image was not strong enough in the community to support a successful capital campaign at the time. It needed to build a much stronger donor support network for a campaign. Reluctantly the board acquiesced and its primary focus instead became a series of outreach activities to build brand in relevant donor communities. This involved creating a corporation that now has 30 members, running a series of cultivation events, and building a stronger development staff. At the end of five years, the CEO reluctantly and correctly assessed they were still not ready, although significant progress had been made. Instead he retired at a normal retirement age, reluctantly leaving the problem to his successor. In all of this, he worked closely with both the chair and the head of the governance committee. The chair concurred with the CEO that a capital campaign was not in order at this time. The governance committee continues to slog through an interminable list of candidates to find donor trustees, connector trustees, and corporators. It is hoped that the museum will be capital-campaign ready in another five years.

Chair of the Governance Committee

Traditionally, the chair of the governance committee is the second most senior and powerful position on the board. This individual is responsible for assembling a board of donors and connectors to enable the organization to both plan its future and have access to the resources needed to achieve that future. Passion, vision, and connections are the keys to successful execution of this role. Every organization described so far has had an activist chair of the governance committee. That person did three things. The first was through the appointment of a search committee to find an energetic and visionary CEO with a desire to rebuild and reposition the organization. No board committee or task is more important than the successful completion of a CEO search. With the right leader in place, the board can subside back into a role of monitoring performance and raising money. The wrong leader can lead to discord, turmoil, and uneven performance, usually followed by all the delays posed by the conduct of yet another search.

The second thing was the successful recruiting and development of a board chair. A good chair begins with a deep passion for the organization, time to do what is normally a very time-consuming job, some personal resources (must contribute significantly but does not need to be the lead donor), and strong interpersonal skills. The chemistry with the CEO is important, particularly because chairs change more rapidly than CEOs.

The third thing was the successful recruiting of a development committee chair. This must be a fearless person who genuinely likes to ask people for money. For the most part, they are high-energy, very positive people. They are rare and hard to find. A key ingredient to almost all the success stories in the first three chapters was an effective head of the development committee who, like a magnet, attracted others to the development task. Effectively filled, these three individuals collectively should be able to drive the organization forward. The remaining job of the governance committee is helping to fill membership with a limited number of donors and connectors

Chairman of the Board

Partially discussed in the previous paragraphs, this person helps to mobilize the broad community behind the organization. The CEO is responsible for developing the organization's strategy and structure for implementing it. The chair is responsible for ensuring the governance committee has carefully evaluated the CEO performance and that of the board. The chair is responsible for communicating the results of this work in a way she thinks is most appropriate. Several important points need to be made:

1. The most sensitive relationship in the organization is that between the chair and the CEO. There are few analogies

between it and prevailing practice in the US private sector. In the private sector, the chairman and the CEO is usually the same person. In the social sector, conversely, the chair is the unpaid boss of the CEO.

2. The relationship between the governance committee head and the chair must also be very tight. They must collaboratively work together to have both an effective governance structure and an optimum climate/support for development.

3. The relationship between the governance committee head and the development committee head has to be very close with each having empathy for the other. The governance committee head must juggle to get the portfolio of skills on the board needed for effective governance (audit, finance, etc.). The development committee head conversely is looking for as many slots for major donors as possible. The development head isn't much concerned with either board size or trustee cultural fit, two items of great importance to the governance committee head.

These are important issues that have to be raised and resolved.

Head of Capital Campaign Committee

When a capital campaign is under way, the chair of the campaign normally sits on the board. The individual's role in that context is to keep the board up to speed on the campaign's progress. Specifically, the chair is also there to nudge them into their pledges and to help make connection with other people. There is particular need for ongoing coordination with the development committee and the development organization to ensure battles between the annual fund and the capital campaign do not occur. Annual fund chairs are almost always concerned about being cannibalized by the capital campaign. More often than not, when capital campaigns are over, annual funds are up as some people just keep giving at a higher level.

Summary

In conclusion, the most effective transformations have come when one or two development-oriented energetic trustees are recruited to the board that can reposition the board's priorities. The common theme in each of the cases described here was strong CEO and development leadership. This came with the active intervention of the head of the governance committee and the active support of the chair. For the museum, deep in the background was a deep-pocketed sponsor who has a passion for it. As long as that individual lives and is vigorous, all is well. The sponsor's children, however, have other passions. The result is a long, drawn-out effort by the museum to attain resources from alternate sources. A new patron and a deep development network are needed.

A happier story was a school. A generous affluent parent correctly assessed the school could help his son prosper. Each year as the school delivered, the parent became more supportive, ultimately inspiring many others to join the effort. Over five years, significant funds were raised, classrooms became full, transfers halved, and college placement soared. At the diocese, it was an outlier gift that was used to motivate others to reach to levels that had previously not been seen to be achievable.

Questions a trustee should ask about the players

- Is the CEO adequately focused on philanthropy for the role it plays in the organization?
- Are the board chair and the head of the governance committee aligned on the number and type of trustees needed to drive philanthropy and the size of the board for the task ahead?
- Is the development director appropriate for the task in front of you? Mix of skills must change over time as needs change. Building capability versus right sizing after a capital campaign are totally different types of tasks, which require different skills.
- Where can I, as a trustee, add value in this constellation?

4

The Annual Fund

A CRITICAL COMPONENT of most social sector organization's development efforts is the annual fund. For many organizations like churches or public-interest-issue groups, it may be their primary source of funds and as such, a matter of major board and CEO focus. Interruptions in its performance can have catastrophic impact on the organization's activities and even survival. At the other extreme lie some hospitals where the annual fund is a useful supplement to the organization's resources, but the hospital's operations are not crippled if there is a shortfall from the budgeted amount of funds to be raised by the annual fund.

Before the start of the year, a revenue target is established for the annual fund together with the estimated sources of these funds (friends, grateful patients, alumni foundations, etc.). Coming up with this number is very much an art. It necessarily contains many assumptions and aspirations that are quite rough in nature. Some of the key inputs to this process include the following.

Last Year's Target and Results

This is clearly the starting point. Did our results diverge significantly from the budget last year and if so, what are the most likely reasons? Had we planned too ambitious a jump from the prior year?

Were there unexpected economic headwinds? Were there special factors impacting the institution such as a major scandal or the unexpected resignation of a key officer such as the CEO? Was there unanticipated turmoil in the development office such as illness, unexpected resignations, and so forth? Careful analysis of the previous year's performance versus budget is the normal place to start in preparing a budget.

Performance Against Similar Organizations

Often, organizations become too inward looking. External comparisons are key and often very sobering. If, for example, a school in a similar area with similar parent demographics is raising twice as much in their annual fund as we are, an obvious question is, why? Has this been a low priority area for us, do we have a staffing or leadership challenge in this area? Do we need an outside consulting firm's assistance in this domain, and so forth.

Are There Special Opportunities This Year?

Are there significantly more or less potential paying members associated with the organization this year? (Program expansion or decrease, enrollment changes, unusual events either positive or negative in our organization, etc.). Do we have remarkably different annual fund leadership in terms of skills and energy on both the staff and volunteer side for the coming year versus the previous year? Are there special events that have occurred in the broader economy that have either stimulated or depressed philanthropic animal spirits? In situations like this, past performance may give little insight for the future. Sadly, when you most need support, the sources may simply dry up (such as a financial meltdown, pandemic, or emerging recession).

Are We Getting the Right Amount from Our Constituencies?

For a church, two measures of success might be the total dollar value of all pledges and the number of families who make a pledge. Is the number of families participating in the annual fund anticipated to rise or fall over last year? Are we getting the right amount of money from the high-end families? In a recent campaign, one family was pledging 2.5 times the next largest gift. The development committee chair was able to use this pledge to get two other families of significant means to jump their pledge up to this new "normal." Are we working at growing the number of families? Sense of community is very important. People with limited resources need to be encouraged to participate and feel that they are full members in a church in every sense. Their very presence helps create vibrancy in the community and should encourage more philanthropy from those who can afford it. Pledging money is only one way to support an organization. Your work as a volunteer is critical as is your presence as an active member of the community.

Other organizations have multiple communities, each of whose contributions in an annual fund need to be tracked separately. A school, for example, often has at least three major giving constituencies—namely, faculty, parents, and alumni. There are, of course, other potential categories such as past parents, friends, grandparents, and so on. Many parents and alumni may see high faculty and staff participation in the annual fund as a positive sign that those closest to day-to-day operations are visibly supportive of the institution. A high number of participants from this group consequently can help stimulate giving from other constituencies.

Parent annual giving for schools is often critical. To drive the support of this constituency, therefore, schools often organize solicitation by class (Grade 1, Grade 2, etc.) and work toward 100%

participation in each class (being sensitive to family economics). In some cases, a $10 gift is more meaningful than a $25,000 gift. Additionally, especially affluent parents may be approached separately from the class effort and solicited by some combination of a member of the development committee, the development director, and the CEO. Additionally, special fundraising efforts are normally made around the graduating class. This is often the last opportunity to secure a major gift from these families as their children move on to college and their parents' attention turns to other philanthropic endeavors and other horizons.

Alumni are often broken into two groups for annual fund purposes. One group is normal every-year annual giving. These are often solicited by mail and by telethons. The other groups are classes coming up on an every-five-years reunion. For schools that go through high school as well as for colleges, the numbers associated with these reunion gifts can be staggering. The author remembers vividly his second day as a freshman at Harvard as he sat in a large amphitheater being told with his 1,100 other classmates that courtesy of the generosity of previous classes (and their gifts to the University's endowment), all in the room were on at least a 50% scholarship. However, the presentation went on to note that at our class's 25th reunion, we would have the opportunity to repay that scholarship. Most people in that room never forgot that warm, early September day speech. At the author's 20th reunion, the class gift was $200,000. However, at the 25th reunion, it jumped to $8 million; and at the 35th reunion, it was $15 million (it was still going strong at his 60th, although most gifts were now planned gifts; see Chapter 6). All of this, of course, needs to be budgeted, which is a very complicated and imprecise process. For example, a year when Bill Gates's class has a major reunion will likely have quite different reunion results than in a year when his class does not have a major reunion.

Lack of insight into an individual's wealth and his or her feeling of warmth to the organization further complicates this. This was first vividly driven home to the author on his 25th university undergraduate reunion, where he served on the major gifts committee. Of the people who the class thought would give major gifts, very few actually did (they came from wealthy families, but had not individually contributed to the growth of that wealth). However, many major gifts came from former scholarship students as well as students from families of modest means at the time they attended the university. These individuals felt the university had opened whole new vistas to them and wanted to give a tangible gift that would allow the university to help the next generation of students like them in the same way. We got the budgeted number of major gifts (and their dollars) but from different people than we had anticipated. Over his life, the author has learned that it is much easier to solicit money from those who have made it than from those who have inherited it. Those who have made it tend to be confident they will make more. Those who have inherited it are often afraid of losing it.

In planning a successful class reunion, the class is normally split apart into two alumni committees, each supported by a different set of institutional officers. One committee and set of institutional officers is the development/class gift group, and the other is the class reunion events committee. The reunion events committee and their officers are charged with producing a wonderful experience for the alumni, filled with nostalgia and visions of the future (see Chapter 7 on events). This experience, in turn, creates a sea of happy alumni for the development/class gift committee and their officers to fish in.

Annual funds are charged with raising the largest amount of money they tastefully can without harming long-term development prospects of individuals where it is too early for them to make a major gift, given their personal circumstances, but where there may be great potential. This is a tricky scenario that must be managed effectively on a case-by-case basis.

Is Our Budget Reasonable Given the Economy?

Annual funds tend to do much better in meeting aggressive growth targets in economic boom times than in periods of economic stress. Interestingly, some studies suggest that reunion classes turn out to be much more generous when they graduated in times of economic prosperity, rather than if they graduated during times of economic distress. For example, in one university, the classes of 1912, 1913, 1914, and 1920 were much more generous in their gifts over the years than the World War I classes, or the Depression-era classes. The general hard times of these eras somehow negatively impacted the view of graduates of those eras.

Annual Fund Staffing Adequacy

Is enough institution staff in place to support the budgeted level of giving? Have we recruited the number and quality of volunteer staff needed to support this level of giving?

Stage of Development of Annual Fund

Is our organization in a relatively mature situation, vis-à-vis the annual fund, or are we in start-up or ramp-up mode? It makes a big difference in what the results can be if one is in a ramp-up mode, rather than in a mature environment.

In short, setting the budget target for the annual fund is a challenging process with no science underpinning it.

Picking the Annual Fund Chair

With the target fixed, the next task is the organizing of the campaign. For all but the largest of social enterprises, the most important task is the recruiting of the volunteer annual fund chair of the effort. If you get this right, almost surely good results will follow. You need a great communicator extrovert, who is energetic, works well with people, is organized, likes to ask people for money, and is not dismayed by rejection. Good annual funds are surrounded by a sense of excitement and a feeling that great days are ahead for the organization. The key person generating that excitement is the head of the annual fund. It is done through speeches, podcasts, social media, one-on-one meetings, telephone calls, written communication, and so forth. All meetings need to have a relentless upbeat tone to them. The world is filled with opportunities, not problems. A steady frame of optimism around a campaign literally becomes self-fulfilling in its infectious permeation of the staff. This job, if well done, is very time-consuming. You need to make sure the volunteer leader has the time to devote to it.

Logistics

Good annual fund campaigns rest on a foundation of well-designed and maintained logistics and database systems. Even the smallest organizations normally have a well-maintained supporter database. This includes names, nicknames, accurate and well-maintained addresses, email addresses, and telephone numbers. Procedures for both culling the database for no longer relevant names and adding new names are important. Past giving histories need to be maintained for everyone. Money spent on software packages for this and data entry staff is money well spent. The scale of effort varies widely. It can range from the church secretary with her Excel spreadsheet extracted from a database package to the processes of large museums and universities, which have multimillion-dollar software packages. (see Chapter 8 for more on this topic).

Campaign Mission and Theme

The first task that the annual fund committee chair and his/her team must do is to identify the major targets that will be supported by this year's campaign and perhaps develop an appropriate tagline, such as

Building for Tomorrow, that can rally solicitors together around an inspirational theme. With the assistance of graphic artists and website designers, an appropriate set of campaign materials can then be prepared for social media, snail mail, and other print media.

Prelaunch Solicitation

Major organization officers, key staff, and all members of the board of trustees should be solicited if possible for their pledges in advance of the annual fund campaign launch. At the formal campaign launch, the commitment of 100% of the trustees and key supporters should be able to be announced. This block of support gives maximum heft to the campaign. The author's view is simple. Any board member who cannot support the annual fund at least at a minimum level should resign. Protests about an organization's policies are always helpful but denying support for the annual fund for an officer or trustee is the wrong way and place to do it. At the time of the public campaign launch of the annual campaign, the number of supporters and the total raised to date are important facts to share and communicate. This data helps radiate that important aurora of self-confidence and success.

Formal Launch

The time of formal launch is normally characterized by kickoff events, speeches, waves of snail-mail postings on websites, creating new websites, and email blasts. These items must present a coordinated message. Graphic artists, content specialists, and campaign facilitators all have their role to play in those communications.

The mission of the annual fund and the intended use of its funds must be clear. Some campaigns allow donors to specify specific projects toward which an individual's gifts can be directed. The author's preference is for general purpose gifts whenever possible. These give the organization maximum flexibility to match funds with needs (anticipated and unanticipated). It also tremendously simplifies stewardship issues.

A key issue addressed earlier is whether you ask for a gift at a specific level based on the person's past giving history and what you have been able to learn about their giving habits. One danger, of course, in asking for a specific gift is that you may not reach high enough, given the individual's capacity. Conversely, an absurdly high request may upset the relationship with the person.

As noted earlier, many organizations have giving societies. Each year, attempts are made by volunteers and development officers to move donors up from one society to the next highest. This is particularly useful in situations where many of the donors know each other as people who want to associate with their peers. A common society is one for younger donors who have graduated in the last decade and have given each year since graduation. Installing that early habit of giving is terribly important. It is often a precursor to major gifts when one has a 25th or 40th reunion. Interestingly, as noted in earlier examples, there are always a few people who want to be recognized for less than they actually gave (either out of privacy issues or to avoid becoming a target for other organizations).

Who and how you approach people is very much a function of their giving history and your perceptions of their wealth. The anticipated high-end gifts are done by the annual fund head or by the chief development officer. These solicitations become very complex if a capital campaign is in the offing or under way. You want an annual fund gift of size on the one hand to support existing operations but on the other hand, you may also want a capital gift, from the same individual, that is one or two orders of magnitude higher. You don't want the person giving the annual gift to think it is a substitute for the capital gift.

When one gets an annual gift that is out of line with expectations on the high side, it needs to be looked at carefully to see if it is a signaling gift. People who want to become closer to an organization often do this. For example, recently a relatively new donor to an organization went from a $5,000 annual gift to a $25,000 gift. A subsequent meeting initiated by the development director revealed the person had become much enamored with the organization and wanted to become much closer, perhaps becoming a trustee. It was also intimated during the meeting that as a trustee, her philanthropic juices might, in fact, run a good deal faster. In short, anything out of the routine is an occasion for reflection and perhaps action. A 50% drop in a gift could be simply changed circumstances or anger about some issues. It needs to be investigated and not left to fester.

An illustrative case with a happy outcome took place several years ago. A parishioner in a local parish lost confidence in the parish and moved to another parish of the same denomination. The parishioner had made a $50,000 capital pledge to the original parish. The parishioner did not want to fulfill it because of concern that it might be totally wasted (which was why he had changed parishes). Fortunately, there was a capital campaign going on in the diocese this parish was part of for a new conference center. The parishioner switched the pledge to the conference center, and felt good about satisfying the pledge to the church broadly defined. He thought nothing more about it.

The outside consultant on the diocesan capital campaign, however, noted this unanticipated large gift from an unknown member of the diocese and decided to investigate. She reached out to the parishioner and found the individual was both committed to the church in general and was an experienced development person with significant personal resources. She arranged a meeting with the parishioner and the presiding bishop of the diocese. The chemistry between the two was so good the parishioner was successively asked to lead the capital campaign to a conclusion, then to head up a new development committee for the diocese, and ultimately to head-up the next diocesan campaign six years later. The individual ultimately gave substantially more to the diocesan campaign than the original pledge to the conference center. Curiosity and follow-up on the nonroutine is important.

Tracking Asks

For significant annual fund donors, the organization's expectations for them are significant, often greater than their past gifts. Overwhelmingly, it is felt to be important by the development professionals to use that "reach" number in a direct solicitation. A recurring problem, however, is that at the last moment, the solicitor blinks and, on their own, substitutes a much lower number. Even more frustrating, they may then lie to you in embarrassment about what was done. Some organizations solicit in teams of two just to avoid this phenomenon. If a solicitor repeatedly comes up short, their supervisor needs to get involved and help. This is a difficult sensitive situation, particularly if the solicitor is a significant donor.

Persistence Is Critical

Multiple waves of contact are often necessary for the annual fund. Letters, emails, and telephone calls are all weapons in a war of attrition. A record must be made of each attempted contact and its success. Without good records, you may inadvertently push harder than is right for the soliciting call of the moment. In all but the most unusual circumstances, when you get a pledge (even if much smaller than you hoped for), you have gone far enough for this year. These are lifelong relationships, and knowing when not to push forward at a particular time is an important skill. Capital gifts and planned gifts will likely be topics for future meetings. Obviously, good management of a prospect involves making a permanent record of the call (and its highlights), plus a thank you note for any gift. Over the long term, these records become very important inputs to capital campaigns and planned giving. These records are key because, often, different people are soliciting for the annual fund than will solicit for a future capital campaign. Each person needs to be informed about the other's activities.

Volunteer Training

This is very important. Volunteers need to know the objectives of the annual fund in great detail and what the relative priorities are of its different components. They need a draft script of their call. The content and tone of interviewing will vary widely from one social enterprise to another and require very different approaches. The ask, for example, for an overseas gap year study program versus for a church could not be more different in tone from each other.

Cold-Call Telethons

Cold-call telethons target small donors who may give only irregularly. For colleges and schools, a participation chair (responsible for getting as wide participation of the classmates as possible) is normally in charge of the telethon. The participation chair is charged with getting all classmates to give at least something. The gifts may run $25 to $100 and be built on nostalgia for the institution (although there is always the occasional surprise). These are relatively easy calls once you make contact. Making contact, however, because of caller ID is much harder today. Calls for money are repeatedly classified as spam and can be easily deleted by the intended recipient. Emails and snail mail are other ways to follow up these calls.

Donors You Know

These are very important but tricky calls. You have a personal relationship with the individual, but you may not know how the individual feels about the institution. The trick is to be positive and not take personally negative feedback about the institution. In difficult cases, the organization may eventually decide to put the person on a no-call list and simply communicate through email and snail mail (over the passage of time perspectives can change). In one case, one of the author's friend's family members was not treated well at all by an institution and the friend vowed never to contribute to it again. Fifteen years later, however, the friend met the new head of the institution who was trying to move the institution in an entirely different direction. In spite of himself, the friend was intrigued by the turnaround and ultimately got deeply involved, both financially and as a board member.

In another case, it may be in abeyance forever. A solicitor received a letter following the annual fund solicitation, saying the person would support the annual fund at a modest level for the indefinite future, but would not be further involved because he did not like the philosophy behind the product. The solicitor left it that when the donor's grandchildren were of age (they were not yet born), they should look again. The product has dramatically changed in the decades that followed since their exchange of correspondence. It remains to be seen, however, whether there will ever be a change in the donor's perspective in this case.

Initial Nonrespondents

The trick is to know who the nonrespondents are and then bring a focused campaign to their solicitation. A recent social service campaign illustrates this. Nearly 500 solicitation packages were initially shipped out by mail. All nonrespondents to this package, who had given last year, subsequently received as follow-up first a telephone message (message left if the person was not at home) and then an email. If that did not work, the remainder of nonrespondents were then divided into 7 clusters of 15 with 7 volunteers assigned (one to each cluster) to pursue them by telephone and mail. Three weeks later, a total of 207 individuals had responded positively. Each remaining nonrespondent was then sent a special delivery FedEx package with a personalized letter in it. Two weeks later, the total pledges had risen to 243, setting a record for the organization in terms of number of gifts. Relentless pursuit of only nonrespondents using the expensive distribution channel of FedEx did the job. Persistence and subsequent aggressive follow-up can make a difference. It must be done tastefully.

Humans Have Habits

A great bane of annual fund heads is that humans are creatures of habit and change can be very hard. If you are used to paying a pledge in April, getting you to do it in January may be almost impossible. More frequent mailings have acerbated this problem because donors afraid of sending three or more gifts each year by mistake may inadvertently wind up sending nothing.

Donor Education

When someone first joins an organization as a member, they usually have very little understanding of how it is financed and what expectations are of an individual in the first several years. Donor transparency for small and midsize organizations is critical. Number of donors, total giving, and giving/donor are pieces of information that donors expect to have today. (They also need transparency on the expense side). Obviously, the data on individual gifts is kept confidential.

Mean gift level, median gift level, and the shape of the giving pyramid are really important things for the development officer to understand. If the largest gift is three times the next largest gift, this could be a real problem if the large gift is a significant part of the total giving. If the lead donor becomes disaffected in some way, the organization becomes vulnerable to having to suddenly retrench. This is not a paranoid thought because the reality is that sometimes people do become alienated from organizations.

One obvious solution to the problem is to find another one or two people to give at the same level as the large gift, thus mitigating the risk of one donor leaving. The reality is that there are much bigger concentrations of wealth today, facilitating the potential success of this tactic. When one person gives at the highest level, it does change the nature of the dialogue with other donors. The author wryly remembers a conversation with an individual who had just heard news of the largest gift ever given to the organization. His thought was that a new norm for meaningful gifts had just been established (in fact, it had).

Emotional Impact

The sad **fact** is that some annual funds are in organizations that are just more viscerally appealing to their donors. Parents and grandparents give to schools because of the great impact they can see the school is having on their children and grandchildren. Alumni give in thanks for what they were given many years ago, which allowed them extraordinary opportunities. Hospitals have research centers that prosper through the gifts of grateful patients and their relatives. Museums conversely have a more cerebral appeal, as do libraries. Finding money for both of these is hard work because they do not pull the same visceral heartstrings. It should also be noted that the Tax Act of 2017 made it very difficult for middle-income families to gain any tax benefit from philanthropy (as they had in the past). This has put a real damper on the annual fund part of philanthropy. Conversely, for the wealthy, the tax advantages for philanthropy were maintained.

Transparency on Sources of Support

Fifty years ago, the funding sources for most social enterprises were not much talked about. It is an enormous advantage for fundraising today that transparency in funding now exists and donors can see both the potential sources of funds and risks for organizations. It used to be that only a very few in an organization would have such an overview.

Tonality

Each annual fund campaign has to capture the spirit, ethics, and values of the organization. A church campaign needs to have the proper air of respect and spirituality in it. A lower-school campaign conversely has to be light and enthusiastic in tone. A hospital campaign needs to have care/compassion, technology, and medical ambiance in it, and so forth. A medical research organization needs a message of hope and progress. All need money but they must go about prospecting for it differently, depending on who they are.

Stewardship

The final, but vital part of the annual fund is the prompt and accurate acknowledgment of the gifts, their immediate deposit, sending a note of thanks together with appropriate acknowledgment of a tax-deductible gift. All this helps produce an image of a well-managed enterprise.

Progress Measurement

From beginning to end, preparation of weekly reports of progress on the campaign this year versus last year (and if meaningful, against budget) are vital.

These reports need to be broken down into appropriate subgroups such as category of gifts, region, and so forth. The campaign is then summarized into number of gifts, total dollar value of gifts, and so forth. This report should hit the CEO's desk every week together with an analysis of variances. This speed and transparency keep the necessary tension of accountability in the organization. It should also trigger corrective action in either the annual fund operations or in expenditures as a whole for the organization (if it looks as though the campaign is coming in well below target). It is another example of the old adage, if you cannot measure it, you cannot manage it. In summary form on a monthly or quarterly basis, these reports go to the board. Of course, any cancellations or defaults on pledges are also reported.

Summary

In summary, the annual fund is the primary financial support engine for many organizations and a vital part of other organizations. From the beginning of an organization's creation, an important aspect of its activities is to build financial strength. The annual fund is an important tool. Planned giving, capital campaigns, and special events are other ways of building this strength. No sensible CEO can afford to take her/his eyes off these risk-mitigation strategies for one minute.

Questions a trustee should ask about the annual fund

Strategic Questions

- How is our annual fund doing relative to those of other organizations? Are its goals well understood internally? (This can vary from over 90% support of the organization's financial support to a much more modest role of 3–5% of the organization's total budget.) Is there a shared understanding of the annual fund's importance among the board and senior management? Is its visibility commensurate with its importance?

Participation Questions

- Are there issues of demographic forces hanging over its future (i.e., a very old donor base)? Is support broad or is it too narrow? If narrow, what can I do to broaden it? This could involve a combination of an increased personal gift, soliciting current donors, or networking new people to the organization, and so forth. Is flow of supporters and volunteers adequate? Where is the next generation of annual fund and development leaders coming from? Am I one of them? (The annual fund is often a normal entry point for a trustee with development skills.) Can I help identify and recruit appropriate trustees to help development?

Logistical/Operational Questions

- Are the annual fund's internal logistical processes high quality and cost efficient?
- Have there been embarrassing logistical errors that need addressing?

Staff Support Questions

- Is staff enthusiastic and motivated? Is there stability or is there high turnover?
- Is turnover an addressable issue?

5

Capital Campaign

ONE OF THE most important tasks of a development organization is the running of a capital campaign. Although they put enormous stresses on the organization, in return, these campaigns often offer transformational possibilities to the social sector organization. New buildings, new product service lines, and endowment are just a few of the potential benefit streams from a successful capital campaign.

Capital campaigns normally require enormous time and energy commitments from the CEO as well as the full endorsement and commitment from the board. Indeed, it is not unusual to increase the size and mix of the board at the time of a capital campaign to bring major donors and connectors closer to the institution to jump-start the effort.

Campaign Feasibility

The beginning of a capital campaign normally starts with a feasibility study to add substance and breadth to what has been up to that point a lot of internal dialogue. This study is usually done by an outside consulting organization, experienced in both helping shape and execute capital campaigns, as well as assessing their potential viability.

Three dominant questions have to be addressed at the start—namely,

1. Is the right CEO in place for a capital campaign?
2. Is the timing right for a campaign?
3. Is the board composition right for a capital campaign?

These questions are not easy to answer. Let me address the CEO question first. At the start of the campaign, the CEO must have a compelling vision for the organization, plus high energy and the ability to relate to donors. For example, one of a major church's dioceses installed a new bishop over two decades ago. Early on, with the advice of senior lay leaders, he launched a capital campaign as a way of mobilizing the diocesan staff and the over 100 churches to work together on a common goal. In an organization that had never done a campaign in living memory, over $10 million was raised for a new conference center to be used as a diocesan camp for inner-city children in the summer and for vestry and minister retreats in the fall, winter, and spring. The campaign was magnificently successful because of the vision and leadership of the bishop. All elements of the diocese rose to support it and in so doing found ways of working together that they had been unable to do before and helped bind them together. The mobilized diocese following the campaign was then able to work on a number of joint projects, cutting across various diocesan departments and parishes. Driven by a charismatic leader, the campaign was transformational.

Fifteen years later, the bishop, now 5 years away from retirement, was persuaded by his lay leaders to use his contacts built up over the last 15 years to launch a second capital campaign to mobilize financial support for a series of outreach and facilities restoration projects that he felt deeply about but had not yet gained financial support for. With the aid of an outside consulting firm and an ad hoc development committee, a capital campaign of tens of millions of dollars was conceived and successfully executed over a five-year period. The timing of his retirement and the accompanying celebration of his bishophood dictated timing of the campaign. Intensely personal in its solicitation strategy, his successor simply could not have done such a campaign for years as he lacked the personal long-term contacts with key donors, connectors, and ministers. Years later, the resulting programs and services enabled by this campaign still impact the life of the diocese.

For a major museum, the opposite situation was true. The CEO, near the end of his career, was ideally poised to lead a campaign in terms of energy and over 20 years of great leadership, and strong support among known donors. Despite his best efforts, as confirmed by outside consultants, however, the depth of the donor prospect pool and the general fundraising environment for this type of organization was just not ready to make such an effort successful. Good leadership was a necessary but not sufficient element for success. Instead, a special endowment/fund was established in the CEO's name to honor his service and a meaningful sum was raised for it. Other long-term steps discussed later in this chapter were taken to prepare the organization for an eventual capital campaign. The timing, however, was just not right for a campaign today in spite of CEO readiness.

For a community health services organization, a different issue emerged. The CEO of over 20 years, very happy in his job, has told the board that he would give two years notice before he would depart. No capital campaign lies in the offing, nor would he be the right person to run one. As a consequence, several board members in frustration have closed their wallets and gotten off the board to focus on more dynamic and needy organizations. They liked the organization, but not the CEO's current priorities and lack of energy. These potential financial resources are gone forever from the organization. People often have trouble dealing with a CEO as a problem until it is too late. In short, CEO readiness and the appropriateness in timing for a campaign are the first two great questions that must be answered in considering a capital campaign.

The third key question is whether the board itself is ready for a campaign. The answer to this question comes in two parts. Are they emotionally ready, and are they financially ready?

Emotional readiness is really important. It is very easy for a board to become complacent and self-satisfied with its performance. This is particularly likely if it is not looking externally and benchmarking its position and performance against similar organizations. Deterioration, in focus, can insidiously creep up on an organization and it gradually becomes noncompetitive. The author watched one organization stay out of normal industry accrediting processes for over 40 years. Lacking focus on good benchmarks, this organization, at one time on the leading edge, slowly over time its practices deteriorated and became at variance with good industry practices. As a result, the number of visitors declined, new exhibits declined, and community image began to decline. Reversing it was very hard, requiring a complete governance overhaul and board restaffing. New trustees, term limits, and other aspects of good governance were key to getting the organization into position for what was eventually a successful capital campaign.

Financial readiness is also important. When a capital campaign is announced, one of the first questions the board needs to answer is are all the board members supporting the campaign with their money and what is the aggregate total of their support. One of the schools studied, in fact, had to postpone its campaign launch for several years until enough board members of means and connector board members were in place to give the necessary energy for a successful campaign launch. In this case, enormous credit went to the earlier board members who noted their inadequacies in this regard and encouraged the recruiting of very different successors appropriate for the task now at hand.

A final issue is that sometimes people must have their horizons lifted. A new normal has to be introduced. In the silent prelaunch phase of a hospital capital campaign, early donors were trying to get away on the cheap with $25,000 gifts (their resources were ample for much larger gifts). It took a $1 million pledge from an unexpected source to get the early donors to go back, reconsider what needed to be done, what they could do, and raise their pledges appropriately. This is especially important in 2020. Over the past 20 years, large amounts of wealth have been generated by a few. This has sharply changed the shape of the social-enterprise-giving pyramid, which is now both much higher and much narrower than in the past.

Gaining appropriate support from the few people at the top of the pyramid is vital for a successful campaign.

Other important items that must be encompassed in the feasibility study, in addition to addressing the CEO readiness, appropriateness of the campaign timing, and board-readiness issues, include the following:

1. A candid analysis of the prioritized needs of the organization and their totality. This analysis, although filled with tension about trade-offs between competing projects, is critical to address and sort out. Sadly, however, legitimate need always surpasses campaign financial targets.

2. The number and readiness of potential supporters of the organization to respond favorably to a campaign. This is the most delicate part of the feasibility study. The potential donors have to both want the project and have the resources to be able to support it. Sometimes you have enthusiastic supporters who have no resources. Other times, the potential donors have the financial resources but are unenthusiastic about this organization and this set of projects at this point in time. How much money can be reasonably raised is a core issue. Candid interviews by a consulting firm with specific donors and their comparison of donor readiness in similar organizations that have done recent campaigns is critical. This analysis led to the correct postponement of the earlier-mentioned museum campaign. The CEO was ready but the climate was wrong. The passionate donor candidates simply were not there in sufficient numbers.

3. Is the social enterprise adequately staffed below the board to support such a campaign? A recent case encountered by the author was a social enterprise that needed to invest and grow heavily to secure its future (its need for funds was unquestionable). However, it had an impecunious and unconnected board plus a development director who didn't have a charismatic bone in his body. It took two years to get these issues resolved including new board members, new board leadership, and a new development director before a capital campaign with significant prospects for success could be launched.

In summary, if the recommendation to proceed with the capital campaign is positive from the consulting company, the board and CEO can decide if it is time to go full steam ahead. The rest of this chapter focuses on what happens if a decision to go ahead is made.

Campaign Setup

Given the decision to proceed, in no particular order, the following things have to happen:

1. **Campaign Chair.** The appointment of the capital-campaign chair. This may well be an appointment of a trustee (or former trustee). The chair must be personally credible, be a significant donor (he/she hopefully is a good connector who can also lead by personal example), and be seen as a person of stature in the relevant communities. This individual will not only make a significant pledge initially, but will likely have to be prepared to do something at the end of the campaign to bring the project across the goal line.

2. **Campaign Steering Committee.** The appointment of a capital campaign steering committee, made up of mostly key potential donors, connectors, and key administrative staff (often the CEO is an ex-officio member). For large campaigns, this will

rapidly expand to regional committees and country committees. As described later, larger organizations often have standing advisory committees whose members can be mobilized to fill out these committees.

3. **Campaign Scope.** The final sizing up of the campaign must be determined. What will be included and what will be excluded? There will necessarily have to be some wiggle room because some major donors will get riveted on something which is worthwhile but not in the plan, and they will be implacable to redirection. The issue sometimes comes down to realizing that it is the only thing the donor wants to fund and in any event, it is a legitimate long-term action. The question becomes you either do it now with this funding source or the source disappears, doing nothing for the institution. The author recently watched a school squash program be launched for just this reason. Since the gift covered all capital expenses and endowment for maintenance expenses, and the organization had the bandwidth administratively to handle the project, it was funded even though it was not in the original campaign scope.

4. **Campaign Director.** The hiring and acculturation of the campaign director. No position is more vital, sensitive, or difficult to fill. (In smaller organizations, this role is usually filled by the director of development.) The complexity of this job is because many of the skills and background needed are in conflict with each other. Key attributes needed include:

   - A highly personable and a self-motivated entrepreneur. The individual is creating an organization where none existed before. The individual must be able to work with both the CEO (as his/her major development counselor) and the trustee head of the development committee (or campaign committee). The campaign director effectively reports to the two of them. The director must also recruit/build a team of major gift officers and other staff to support the campaign (to the extent they are not already in the organization).

- Quickly resolving whether the leader is to come from outside the organization. Someone who has done campaigns before in other settings brings real advantages. She will exude credibility with her insight from past campaigns and will have an innate sense of pace borne from personal experiences about how fast you can move. She also will have a network of advisors and people who have worked with her on previous campaigns that she can mobilize. Finally, she has tasted success (or you would not be considering her). On the other hand, someone recruited from within understands the organization culture and hopefully the major donors very well. She will know how to mobilize the right internal resources for each individual donor. She can get started much faster. There is no right answer in general to this question. Three examples the author has recently observed, however, highlight the importance and complexity of getting the right development head. A school of nearly 1,000 students launched its first capital campaign in 40 years. An outside development leader was brought in because the internal resources were simply not there at the school. Highly personable, she was able to immediately bond with the chair of the board, the CEO, and the key board members on the newly formed development committee. Working with the board, she planned and implemented major development events for curated parents and friends of the school, where the school's vision was laid out by both the head and the board chair. These types of events had never been done before. These group meetings were followed by personal meetings with key potential donors. These meeting always included the CEO. Buttressed by the support of key lead donors from a newly constituted board, nearly 50% of the campaign total was raised from the board. That success allowed her to approach affluent parents with the organization's head to finish off that campaign. She then drove an even larger campaign two years later, targeted at a very different cluster of parent donors who were interested in very different projects than those covered in the initial campaign. Development staff was completely repopulated with none having been there three years earlier.

A major, over-100-year-old hospital approached its capital campaign in a different way. It had been nearly 10 years since the previous capital campaign. A new development director from outside the hospital was recruited to replace the recently retired development director. Over the first year, he worked with the CEO, the board, key physician leaders, and his internal staff to define a capital campaign for new technology and facilities that fit the future needs of the hospital. In this effort, two long-term development officers supported him. Those two development officers had participated in the previous campaign, as well as annual fund activities, and knew the history of their donor base. The new director also mobilized the development office to find a whole new set of donors. They began by identifying all households within 10 miles whose assessed property values were of a specific size or higher. This was then matched with a list of known patients of the hospital. It turned out that the hospital's reputation in the community (confirmed by a campaign feasibility study) dramatically exceeded the hospital's knowledge of its base of friends. For example, nearly half the residents of a nearby up-market retirement center either had had continuing-care relationships with the hospital or had had surgical procedures done there in the past five years. None had been approached for development events. In this case, a new director brought additional energy and insight to an existing organization and moved it forward by both capitalizing on existing relationships and opening new ones. Thirty-year donors were combined with brand-new capital-campaign donor prospects.

The third example is the previously mentioned museum that desperately needs a campaign, but does not have the image yet in the community to support one. Consequently, the new director of development is in friend-raising mode. This has meant first ensuring potential supporters are brought onto an appropriately term-limited board. At the end of their term, they are graduated either onto the role of trustee emeritus, member of the corporation (newly formed) that meets twice a year, member of one of the seven ad hoc advisory committees around specific programs, or they join (or stay on) one of the board standing committees. In addition each year, they are asked to help support one of the outreach gala events in both an organizing capacity and attending capacity (more in Chapter 7 on events). Additionally, in the second year of their second three-year trustee term, each trustee now has a specific meeting with the CEO and chair to talk about their desired future involvement with the organization upon completion of their trusteeship. Finally, a planned giving committee and a planned giving program have been established and introduced to all trustees and corporators. Much progress has been made, but realistically, it will be up to five or more years before a capital campaign with strong prospects for success will be possible for the organization. The new CEO has been recruited with the expected skill set to deal with this.

In two of these examples, the campaign director was the critical lynchpin for an eventual successful campaign. In the third case, the development director is building the infrastructure for an eventually successful campaign.

5. **Campaign Duration.** The length of the campaign is heavily influenced by the nature of the organization. Schools are interesting because every year, a new group of students and their parents (new prospective donors) enter. Some parents are very generous in the first couple of years because they know their child will personally benefit from the expenditures made during this time. In the final year of the child's enrollment, the parents may also make a gift in gratitude for their child's experience. Thereafter, however, the probability of a gift drops sharply as the parents transition to other interests. This means that

capital campaigns for a school should be spaced no more than five or six years apart if parents are a major part of the donor pool (versus alums). Conversely, in hospitals and museums, there is no such periodicity. Hospitals depend heavily on grateful patients, or parents thereof (the actuarial tables, however, suggest relatively frequent campaigns). Museums often get gifts of art later in a donor's career as people look to find homes for their collections. Donors to museums often surface in their late 50s and 60s, as college obligations are gone, and their interests deepen (often their resources as well) into areas such as the arts and they reach peak asset-accumulation years. Such organizations tend to do a series of closely spaced capital campaigns. Campaigns longer than five years tend to drag and become stale. It is time to wrap up and immediately start the planning for a new campaign. The reality in 2020 is the majority of time most organizations are in some form of capital campaign.

Silent Phase

With the campaign staffed and its objective refined, the silent phase of the campaign begins. For a large campaign, this phase can easily last several years during which time 50–60% of the total goal of the campaign will normally be raised. In these early days, the following important tasks must be accomplished:

1. **Campaign Statement.** Preparation of the campaign mission statement and the key outputs from the campaign. For even the smallest campaign, multiple buckets must be defined to deal with the different tastes of the donors. The author's first capital campaign nearly 40 years ago taught him a valuable lesson. It was for a very small school (K-6). The campaign was to fund 20 desktop computers, a big outdoor climbing toy for the younger children, and a set of up-market music instruments. Every potential donor would get excited about one of those

investments, could sort of understand the reason for the second, and had no interest in the third. A portfolio of different projects was needed to appeal to different donors. The same is true for large university campaigns at the other end of the size spectrum, which cover buildings, research programs, student scholarships, endowed professorships, athletic programs, and so forth. The key is to convince a donor to support as broad a range as possible of these opportunities.

The ideal donor, of course, from the development office's perspective, is the one who is willing to give a totally unrestricted gift. The unrestricted gift can be used to fill in all the unglamorous, but necessary, infrastructure investments that no one wants to fund, such as parking garages. These are necessary investments, but they stir no one's soul.

2. **Major Donor Prospects.** Preparation of a list of potential major donors who have the capacity and the inclination to give a major transformational gift is a key task. Some are new to your organization. Some are in your orbit and have already given significant gifts in the past. Some people, however, if they are really excited about your mission, will want to give additional previously uncontemplated major gifts. If the relationships have been architected well, future gifts beyond this campaign will ultimately impact their estate plans. Some donors have deep relationships with the institutions, which is why they give. However, others give because they have confidence that a particular institution can deliver on something such as a specific research program, which they believe can contribute mightily to society.

An example is Steve Schwarzman's gift of $333 million to MIT's new center on artificial intelligence, an institution with which he had no previous affiliation. He was, however, deeply interested in artificial intelligence and believed MIT was the right place for a gift of this magnitude to make maximum impact on artificial intelligence research. This is in contrast to his $150 million gift to Yale (of which he is an alumnus) for its new technology-enabled campus center, which is aimed at dramatically improving its undergraduate life.

3. **Gift Cultivation.** Cultivation of major gifts must commence immediately. Many of these relationships, of course, precede this campaign and hopefully will be there for future campaigns long after this one is completed. Normally, a series of brainstorming events are held around the country (and world) to generate both ideas for new donors and enthusiasm among previous donors for the campaign. At an appropriate time, the board of trustees will have a retreat as part of its process of eventually approving a capital campaign. Several new trustees who have a particular interest in one or more segments of the campaign may be added to the board. Others may not have the time to serve on the board, but are willing to serve on a special campaign advisory committee to the CEO. Always, the focus is to try to broaden the network of potentially meaningful supporters.

4. **Materials Preparation.** The preparation of the materials for when the campaign goes public is a big task. Brochures, videos, social media strategies, all must be worked out. News releases and magazine articles will also be part of the campaign. Included in this is the time-phased orchestration of a series of gift announcements to give credibility to the campaign. Depending on the size of the organization and the campaign length, this may involve a great deal of work and buildup of staff.

5. **Extended Donor Outreach.** Extension of donor outreach to people beyond your current donor networks. As the following examples show, you do not know a prospect's potential until you ask.

   ■ A church was doing a capital project for a total building, refurbishing and installation of a new elevator. Total projected expenses were well over $1 million. The minister asked a potential donor who had never given a capital gift for $50,000. The answer was brief and affirmative. In a previously described diocesan capital campaign, an 85-year-old parishioner (unknown in philanthropy circles) was asked by the bishop to give a gift of $100,000. Without blinking, he said "I can do that," and he did.

- A wealthy, but somewhat remote, potential donor to a museum was asked to match $1 million given by someone he thought did not remotely have that kind of wealth. Startled and touched after checking the validity of the gift he was asked to match, he matched it.

The author learned from these incidents to never make assumptions and to always ask for the gift. Unexpected donors can come out of nowhere, whereas those who are heavily counted on sometimes do not come through at all. Inelegantly stated, after all the hard work, there is still risk a meaningful pledge will not come through. You have to hope the law of averages works out.

6. **Creatively Engage Prospects.** Particularly interesting situations arise when the donor wants to make a gift but is searching for something novel. A memorable one to the author was from a philanthropically oriented alum of a college who wanted to make a $15 million gift that would be anonymous but that would make a real difference. The college suggested he underwrite 10 chairs for nontenured faculty at $1.5 million each. The development office could then sell the naming rights for the 10 chairs at $2.5 million to alums who wanted to endow named chairs but could not afford the normal price of $4.0 million for a chair. The alum was excited to leverage his gift this way. Only six months later, all 10 chairs had been funded by alums who were delighted to fund chairs in their names that they thought they could not afford. It was a great success for all 11 donors, helping the college to attract new faculty of the right caliber.

7. **Planned Gift.** For older donors, a popular approach is to give face value credit for a planned gift versus its lower present value. This means the alum gives a gift of $100,000 for a planned annuity (see Chapter 6). The present value of the gift may be $70,000 but the alum is thrilled to get credit in the class report for $100,000 and thus makes a gift larger than he might otherwise have made and feels good about it.

All this suggests that there is a great deal of art to soliciting major gifts. It is also very hard work. Steve Schwarzman vividly describes in his book[1] how hard it was to raise the $400 million beyond his $100 million contribution to the founding of the Schwarzman Scholars Program at Tsinghua University. He talks about the 2,000 customized letters over five years. Many of these were not cold calls, but people whom he knew and had a relationship with. Fundraising is hard, even for billionaires.

Public Phase

The end of the quiet part of a capital campaign is normally at the 50–60% completion level. The public part usually begins with big kickoff events to celebrate success to date and define the path going forward to engage new potential target donors. The trick in these events is to capture the feel of a great emerging success that people want to join and be part of. The key parts of the public phase include the following:

1. Continued solicitation and closure of prospects unearthed and started on in the quiet phase, but not yet completed.
2. The aggressive pursuit of smaller gifts than those pursued in the quiet phase. For example, if the quiet phase was focused on

---

[1]Stephen A. Schwarzman, *What It Takes: Lessons in the Pursuit of Excellence* (Simon & Shuster, 2019).

gifts over $100,000, this phase would include gifts of $100,000 down to $5,000 or lower. Matching gifts and challenge gifts are weapons used at this stage to encourage giving from people perched on the sidelines who can get excited to have their gifts leveraged. The author particularly likes cliff challenges. A cliff challenge is one in which, after donations have reached $15 million, the next $5 million are matched on a dollar-for-dollar basis by the challenge. This approach helps people to stretch high, particularly at campaign closing time.

Names on donor plaques or named seats in an auditorium for a specific price are frequently used tools at the end of a campaign. Naming is a complex and thorny topic. Different organizations have different views about everything from the bathroom sinks on up having names on them. Some love it, whereas others dislike it, believing excessive naming cheapens the whole project.

3. A series of smaller receptions for potential donors. It is tricky to curate the invitation lists for these events. People may feel snubbed by not being invited to the high-end events or alternatively embarrassed by being invited to these high-end events and then being solicited for gifts far beyond their potential capacity.

4. Always be open and friendly. You never really know what people's circumstances are or when circumstances change. The author still recalls a phone call a decade ago from his annual fund director to get a recent contributor of $500,000 on his schedule within the next 24 hours (the time the donor was on campus).

The individual had graduated 30 years earlier from the university. Shortly after graduation, he had founded with his spouse a company in which they held 100% of its stock. Since it was a privately held company, alumni records showed no indication of personal wealth. All their money was tied up in totally illiquid stock of indeterminate value. He had always showed up at every five-year class reunion, never giving more than $100. Six months earlier, he and his spouse sold the company. Out of the proceeds of the sale, they decided to make a gift of $500,000 to the place where they felt it all began (somewhat later that was increased to include a $7 million endowed chair). The message is clear!! You must be friendly to everyone because you do not know where the pockets of wealth are, or where they will be in the future. Sadly, of course, some hoped-for great pockets of wealth either turn out to be empty or tightly sealed.

Large social enterprises often have sophisticated research departments with search engines looking for initial public offerings (IPOs), hedge-fund transactions, and so forth, that might involve someone associated with their institution. In this spirit, the author tirelessly examines each day donor lists of other organizations for traces of philanthropy from individuals who have a link with the institutions he is involved with.

5. Ethical issues are really important. You must carefully understand from whom you are receiving money to ensure they are the kind of people that you are pleased to have your name associated with in the newspapers. The 2020 problems that MIT and Harvard had in dealing with the earlier-mentioned Jeffrey Epstein's gifts and his presence on their campuses is the stuff of nightmares. Particularly sad are names like Sackler, which used to stand for art and integrity, but is now seen as a malignant engine of the opioid crisis. You must be especially careful because the incentive systems for major gifts officers often relate to the volume of money raised by them and does not focus on the source's potential reputational risk. It is vital that there be an ethics check on major gifts done by a disinterested third party. Shear lust and unchecked animal spirits can get you into real trouble.

6. Always keep the donor's perspective in mind. It can be very different from yours. For example, what may seem to be a large gift to you could almost be a throwaway gift from their perspective! The author thinks of one organization getting a regular

$10,000/year contribution for over a decade from an alienated former supporter who saw it as a throwaway token. In reality it was a very welcome addition to this relatively small organization's coffers. In another more dramatic case, a donor of $100 million gift to another organization gave the author's social enterprise a throwaway $10 million (larger than any gift they had ever received—and needless to say, a very welcome one).

Ending the Campaign

At some point, a decision needs to be made on ending the campaign. Reasons for closing it down include the following:

1. Its financial goals have been met or surpassed.
2. All credible solicitable donors have been run through.
3. The overhead costs of the campaign have become high in relation to the benefit stream. It is time to right size the development staff.

In closing down a campaign, important issues to be dealt with include:

1. Make sure that a structure and staff are in place to ensure that all pledge commitments are followed up and collected. Ten percent or more of pledges is not abnormal shrinkage if proper attention is not paid.
2. Campaign files need to be merged with those of the overall development department. Annual fund appeals, reunions, and the next capital campaign for these donors all lie in their future. The data from this campaign will help improve future solicitation efforts. The organizational memory contained in these files is an invaluable and yet easily perishable asset. The author has watched with dismay as a remarkably effective development operation under one CEO simply atrophied under neglect by the subsequent CEO, including disposing of prior

donor records. An organization under great pressure to begin with because of its industry is now in a much more vulnerable position because of institutional neglect of its development assets. At the core was the failure of the new CEO appointment process to put proper weight on this category of skills for the CEO. The CEO is so important for development. In the earlier-mentioned example, at Harvard, when Larry Summers stepped down as president, an about-to-be-launched multibillion-dollar capital campaign was almost instantaneously postponed for several years. (Donors crave stability in leadership to ensure promises will be kept.)

3. An appropriate series of celebratory events need to take place. The timing and nature of these events act as a catalyst to ensure the final solicitations are completed. If the campaign is falling short of its goals, these events provide an opportunity to resolicit the initial donors. Sometimes this closing effort requires a new development committee chair to drive the process forward. This is both because these high-stress volunteer jobs have a real burnout factor and the fact that closeout leadership skills are different than start-up ones. A closing banquet is a wonderful opportunity for the announcement of a surprise capstone gift.

For example, several years ago, a $30 million campaign for a school was brought to a triumphant close with a surprise $2 million gift by the campaign co-chair at the closing celebratory banquet. It was electrifying. In the spirit that no good deed should go unpunished, three years later the donor became co-chair of the next campaign, which resulted in a building with his name on it, among other things.

Conclusion

In truth, in healthy situations, one capital campaign invariably begets another. Specific projects change, leaders change, but the need for investable resources is almost insatiable. We have moved to a world where healthy organizations are in a perpetual capital campaign process either opening one, doing one, or wrapping up one. If you do not like to do this, your future as a successful non-profit CEO is at risk. If you are a board member, both your resources and solicitation skills will forever be in demand.

The author has learned from these incidents to never make assumptions and always ask for the order. Unexpected donors can come out of nowhere while heavily counted-on ones sometimes do not come through at all. Only by asking can you bring closure.

Questions a trustee should ask about a capital campaign

- Why are we doing a campaign at this time? Impending retirement, burning operational priorities, building sustainability, and so forth.
- Is there a universe of potentially supportive donors? Can they be tapped in this timeframe? Who made this assessment and what data did they collect to support it?
- What are the key components of the campaign? Why are they there?
- How critical is this campaign to our survival and ability to give services? Are we sliding downward toward mediocrity and irrelevance?
- What can I personally bring to the campaign? These might include financial resources, network of contacts, credibility, passion, and so forth.
- Is this organization and mission #1 or #2 in my personal priorities? Can I make it such a priority?

6

Planned Giving and Foundations

INDIVIDUAL GIVING OF cash and tangible assets is the lifeblood of financial support for most social enterprises. It is true that cash in hand is better than cash on the way. However, planned giving represents deferred receipt of cash that well might not be otherwise accessible. It is important to note that in the United States, because of our aging demographics, we are in the midst of the largest intergenerational transfer of wealth in US history. Planned giving is a critical weapon in ensuring social enterprise gets its share of this wealth.

There are, however, other forms of philanthropy than individual giving. For example, nearly 20% of philanthropic support for social enterprise today comes in the form of foundation grants. Both the board and the development organization need to be prepared to access this source to the extent possible. Additionally, corporate support amounts to 5% of philanthropic support for social enterprises. Corporate support has become much harder to get over the past several decades. Vendor support for events plus special situation grants where there is marketing synergy are the most frequent occasions in which corporate support is being successfully accessed.

Planned giving is the most technically complicated area of philanthropy from both the donor's and the recipient's viewpoint. This is because many of its tools require complex legal documents, actuarial tables, and forecasts of a donor's future cash needs. Most of its tools are primarily relevant for donors in their 60s and beyond. Planned giving is, of course, closely linked to the donor's estate planning and thus requires strong legal inputs. Effectively done, planned giving officers at social enterprises can raise large sums of money for the organization. Realistically, however, much of its arrival is deferred years into the future. Effective use of planned giving tools allows donors to fine-tune the timing of cash receipts to meet their anticipated ongoing personal needs while being generous philanthropically. Planned giving at its core helps direct money to designated social enterprises that would otherwise go to local and federal tax authorities. Inheritance taxes, capital gains taxes, and income taxes can be avoided by giving assets and income streams to social enterprises using one or more of the vehicles described later. Planned giving in short helps donors dispose tax efficiently of a portion of the personal financial surplus created over their lives through work, saving, and investing to social enterprises. These are assets that the donors have decided are not needed to maintain either the donors' life styles or those of the donors' heirs. Needless to say, these decisions often involve very delicate and emotional issues that take time for donors to think through.

Fortunately, from the viewpoint of social enterprises, the US tax laws are, in general, designed to encourage philanthropy both during and after a donor's life. This, of course, does raise an important cautionary note—namely, that tax laws continuously change. The objectives of a finely tuned set of planned gifts by a donor can be partially or totally thwarted with the stroke of a legislative pen. For example, the US Tax Reform Act of 2017 has caused some people to think about certain aspects of planned giving in quite different ways, because new incentives were added while some old ones were eliminated. The same was true of the American Relief Bill of 2020. Here, certain IRA distribution strategies that once made sense pre-2020 no longer make the same economic sense. This means a professional must periodically review a donor's planned giving strategy to make sure it still makes sense. A donor cannot just do it once and think the subject is closed and never to be revisited.

This chapter provides an overview of US planned giving options. It describes key techniques and provides an overview of the donor situations where they are most appropriate. Before using a specific set of techniques, a donor must retain a specialist to guide them through the intricacies proposed by a social enterprise's planned giving officer. This chapter necessarily is a generalist introduction to an area of great complexity. The devil is in the details. The chapter does not attempt to cover all the nuances or underlying complexities. (That would require several books.) Its objective is to raise new options for a donor to consider. It is important to note, of course, that some aspects of current laws may have changed since this book was written.

An important aspect of many planned giving tools is that they require someone other than the donor to manage a portion of the donor's financial resources that the donor will continue to have an interest in. Therefore, identifying and retaining a quality asset manager for these assets is critical for the donor. The donor must clearly understand their fees in advance. In addition to independent asset managers, major social enterprise organizations like Harvard University not only allow you to use their endowment manager (the Harvard Management Company) to manage the resources that you have given to Harvard through planned giving (assets in which you still have a beneficial interest) but also allow charitable remainder trusts (for example) managed by them to have up to 50% of their assets ultimately designated for social enterprise organizations other than Harvard. This means the donor does not have to worry about the quality of investment managers of the smaller social enterprises they donate to. They can, instead, piggyback planned gifts to these smaller organizations beside a planned gift to Harvard, knowing the assets of this portfolio of gifts will be professionally managed.

A central theme of this chapter is that many forms of planned giving are built on the concept that by taking a little bit from the donor's heirs, the donor can give a lot to social enterprise. The major intended loser in this transaction is the taxing authorities (federal, state, and city). It should be noted that planned gifts could be credited to either the annual fund or capital campaign of a social enterprise.

The chapter describes five major classes of specific planned giving tools. The first class of planned giving tools is the individual retirement account (IRA). The next two tools are, respectively, the charitable remainder trust and the charitable lead trust. The fourth tool is the charitable annuity. A fifth quite different tool is a donor-funded foundation. As will be described, these foundations can range from the small (roughly two-thirds of the foundations in the United States have less than $1 million in assets) to the truly large foundations like the Bill and Melinda Gates Foundation. Foundations, their creation, operation, and grant strategy are complex and specialized topics that warrant a book of their own. They are only relatively briefly discussed here to acknowledge their important role in philanthropy.

Traditional Gift Approaches

Before tackling planned giving vehicles, a few words need to be said about tax efficient normal giving by donors. Four topics are covered here, including cash gifts, appreciated stock, bequests, and life insurance.

Cash Gift Issues

The most traditional way to donate to a social enterprise is simply a cash gift. The donor writes a check and is given a receipt. The donor then uses the receipt to document the tax deduction the donor can take on their federal tax returns for the gift. The US Tax Reform Act of 2017 eliminated this federal tax deduction for most Americans. A taxpayer no longer itemizes charitable deductions on their federal tax return unless the sum of their state and local taxes (capped at $10,000), mortgage interest, and charitable giving add to more than $24,000. This has had a chilling impact on small donations from $10 to $2,000 as the effective cost of these gifts has gone up to their donors who have reacted in many cases by cutting the size of their pledges. For large donors, however, whose combined annual state and local taxes, mortgage interest, and charitable giving in aggregate exceed the $24,000 cap, their incentive to give to social enterprises remained intact. This had led to charitable giving pyramids for social enterprises being both higher (a few really large gifts) but narrower at the base (not so many smaller gifts). The author speculates that when there is a change of federal administration and US Senate control, this state of affairs could well be reversed by new tax legislation.

Appreciated Stock

A more tax-efficient way than giving cash to a charity is giving appreciated stock (assuming the donor has appreciated stock). The charity gives the donor full credit for the total amount of their gift. The donor, however, avoids paying the capital gains tax on the appreciated stock part of the gift. This allows a donor to get greater impact from a stock gift of the same size as a cash gift. All but the smallest charities have established brokerage relationships to handle these stock transactions. Stock gifts from a donor's IRA, of course, incur no taxable capital gains.

If the donor likes the stock that was given to the social enterprise, the donor, of course, can then buy more of it. Hopefully, this stock will also appreciate in future years, laying the basis for yet another stock gift to the social enterprise. If the donor is near the $24,000 level of deductions, described in the previous section, the donor may want to combine two years of charitable gifts into one gift either on December 31 of one year or on January 1 the following year in order to get a tax deduction. Tax advice from a professional should be sought before pursuing this option.

Bequests

Another traditional way of making a gift is to include the social enterprise in the donor's will, either for a specific amount or as a percentage of the estate. The advantage of doing it this way is that the donor has ownership of the asset throughout his or her life as well as control of the asset's income stream. A disadvantage, of course, is that the donor forgoes the tax benefits offered by the techniques described in this chapter and the social enterprise does not get access to any part of the bequest until the donor passes.

In thinking about making a bequest of a specific amount versus making a bequest as a percentage of an estate, interesting complexities can arise. When a donor makes a specific amount bequest, the donor may feel very generous because of the size of the concrete number. However, a donor (irrationally) may not feel emotionally the same way about a percentage of the estate gift, whose actual number might actually be much larger. For example, one of the author's friends, some years ago, received a $5,000 bequest from a relative. He was very touched until a year later, he learned that the other heirs had convinced the relative, shortly before her death, to rewrite her will from giving him 5% of her estate to a gift of $5,000. The other heirs told the relative that this way she could be sure my friend got something substantial (in reality, 5% of the estate, however, would have been $100,000). Ever since, the author has been partial to percentage interests. A danger in putting the percentage interest in your will is that you may forget it is there. Over the years, your priorities change, but this neglected (often forgotten) clause remains operative, perhaps piling up enormous gains to beneficiaries that the donor may not have intended.

Life Insurance

Life insurance is another useful tool for deploying assets to social enterprise. Donor during their lifetimes pay premiums that are non–tax deductible on life insurance policies they own. When the donors pass, if a social enterprise is the beneficiary of the life insurance policies, it will receive the face amount of the policy. This payment of the face value of the policy to the social enterprise takes place outside the settlement process of the estate and as such is not taxable to the estate. Advice from specialists should be sought when making these gifts to ensure the intended results occur.

Major Planned Giving Tools

IRA (Individual Retirement Account)

The IRA (created by the US Congress) was originally conceived of as a retirement savings tool. It works as follows. Each year an individual can put up to $25,000 of their earnings into an IRA (the individual pays no taxes on this part of their earnings). Further, together with the hoped-for investment gains occurring on the assets inside the IRA over the years, this money only becomes taxable to the individual when it is distributed to the individual (distributions must start after one reaches age 70.5). Most people in their early and middle years, as they contribute to the IRA, only think of the IRA as future retirement income.

However, as one becomes older and other sources of retirement income emerge for an individual, such as Social Security, pension plans, and savings, the IRA may no longer be a needed source of retirement income. Instead the IRA can be reconceived as an asset, whose disposition, in part or as a whole, to social enterprise will have no taxes paid on it (assuming 100% goes to social enterprises). Done correctly, this means significantly more money can get to social enterprises than through direct bequests. How?

When an individual established their IRA, the idea was to defer current income (and the tax dollars the individual would have to pay on it) until the individual started taking distributions from the IRA. These distributions would then be taxed to the individual at their current tax rate. As noted earlier, a normal IRA (as opposed to a Roth IRA, which will be described later) requires that the individual start making a minimum annual distribution at age 70.5 (the amount is defined in the US tax tables). If on the individual's death, there are assets left in their IRA and the individual wants to give them to their heirs, the assets in the IRA will be taxed as income to the heirs at their marginal income tax rate. In addition, before the 2017 tax act, the owner's estate first had to pay an inheritance tax on the IRA balance at the estate's marginal inheritance tax rate. The remainder of the IRA was then taxed at the heirs' marginal income tax rate, including both federal and local taxes. This double taxation sharply reduced the size of the assets the heirs got. The inheritance tax feature is currently out of the tax code, courtesy of the 2017 Tax Act. It would not surprise the author, however, if the federal inheritance tax reemerged sometime in the next decade as part of "tax reform" legislation.

Importantly, at an individual's death, if the IRA money is distributed from the IRA to one or more social enterprises directly, no taxes are paid. All the money goes to the social enterprises. This means the individual can give significantly more money to the social enterprise from an IRA than can be given to the individual heirs, who have to pay taxes on it. This is clearly an important estate-planning tool.

Another approach that benefits social enterprise is to distribute portions of an IRA during one's lifetime (after age 70.5) to social enterprises through what is called an IRA qualified distribution. At any time during a year up to $100,000 can be given directly from the IRA to a social enterprise, paying no tax on it at all. In this way money is removed from one's estate with the donor avoiding taxes on the distribution.

A variant of this is the Roth IRA. A Roth IRA has very different tax features than the regular IRA. For the Roth IRA, each year, an individual can put into the IRA up to $6,000 of after-tax income ($7,000 after age 50). This is money the individual has already paid taxes on. Money may be drawn out after age 59.5. No taxes at all are due at the time of withdrawal (i.e., all appreciation and earnings inside the IRA are tax free). Unlike the regular IRA, there is no minimum distribution requirement. Distributions from a Roth IRA to a social enterprise are tax advantaged (because the appreciation that occurs inside the IRA is not taxed), but it is not as tax advantaged as the normal IRA (which avoids taxes on income at the time money is put into IRA).

The key point of this discussion is that an IRA is much more than just a retirement stream provider. It can be reconceived at great advantage as being a tax-advantaged asset for social enterprise distribution. Its ultimate use in this way is, of course, very different from the reason it was originally created by the donor—namely, to generate retirement income.

Irrevocable Charitable Remainder Trust

This is a common planning tool that transfers a piece of a donor's capital to the social enterprise. People who wish to have late-in-life income but believe they will not ever need access to this piece of capital can use this tool. When an irrevocable charitable remainder trust is set up, the following things happen:

1. The donor gets an immediate tax deduction, which is taken in the year the trust is established. Actuarial tables determine the size of the deduction. The deduction is a function of the donor's age (and the age of the donor's spouse if he/she is also an income beneficiary), and the amount of the annual-distribution payment. It is an irrevocable trust. Once created, it cannot be modified either as to terms or its non–social enterprise beneficiaries. If a donor funds the trust with appreciated stock, an additional positive feature is that the donor avoids the capital gains tax that would otherwise have had to be paid on the appreciation part of the stock gift. Also, since it is in an irrevocable trust, its assets are protected from any creditors.

2. The donor receives income from the trust in either of two ways. One is an annual payment based on a fixed percentage of the assets of the trust at the end of the year. If the money is well invested, the payout should rise year after year and can act as an inflation shield. Alternatively, the donor can take a fixed amount per year in which case the trust is called a charitable remainder annuity trust. The payout rate can run from 5% to more than 50% of the initial market value.

3. This trust gives a donor an income stream for either the life or the lives of the donor and spouse, depending on how it is set up. This income stream supplements other retirement income and allows the donor to maintain spending flexibility. It also removes assets from the donor's estate, thereby reducing inheritance taxes.

4. At the donor's choice, the donor can also leave money that would otherwise be distributed annually to them (and be taxed) in the trust and allow it to build up over time. Taxation on this undistributed income is avoided until it is distributed to the donor.

5. Although the trust is irrevocable, the donor has the flexibility to change the social enterprise beneficiaries during the donor's life (to other qualified social enterprises). The donor may not add, however, non–social enterprises as beneficiaries. The donor may have multiple social enterprise beneficiaries for the same trust. This is very helpful if the donor has one large social enterprise beneficiary and several smaller ones. The large social enterprise beneficiary manager is often willing to manage the entire trust (like the earlier mentioned Harvard Management Company example).

6. Selection of the investment manager for the trust is a very important decision. The donor needs to study the alternatives carefully. In many cases, people build in the flexibility to change the manager, so if there is poor performance or if the donor does not like the individual in charge, the donor can move on to another investment manager. A donor can even

decide to become the investment manager. A donor, however, has to be careful in this case to meet certain regulatory guidelines or otherwise tax deductibility will be lost.

7. If the donor wishes, the trust can be structured so that, after both the donor and spouse pass, their children may become income beneficiaries and the trust can run for another generation.

At the core, the charitable remainder trust is a way to make a generous and meaningful equity gift to social enterprises while continuing to receive income during the donor's lifetime (and that of the donor's spouse). It is a win-win with the organization getting a non-revocable gift (although not immediately accessible for spending purposes) and the donor getting retirement income. Again, this is an instrument that requires competent legal and financial planning input to set up. It also needs professional money-management skills to make sure it provides the proper returns.

Irrevocable Charitable Lead Trust

In many ways, this is the exact reverse of the irrevocable charitable remainder trust. This is a vehicle for a donor who has no need for additional retirement income but wants to preserve control over the ultimate distribution of their capital until the time of their passing. When an irrevocable charitable lead trust is set up, the following things happen:

1. The donor gets an immediate tax deduction to be taken in the year of the trust's establishment. It is an irrevocable trust and once established cannot be modified other than that the social enterprise beneficiaries may be changed. The calculation of the tax deduction is complicated because it takes into account a number of factors. These include the IRS's interest rate on asset growth, the projected payment each year, and various other terms of the trust.

2. Payments are made at least annually to a social enterprise either for a fixed number of years or for the lives of one or more persons.

3. At the end of the trust term, the assets are distributed to the non–social enterprise beneficiaries.

4. The payments (at least annual) may be of two types. One is called a lead annuity trust, where a fixed amount, typically the same for each year, is paid annually. A variant is a lead unitrust, where a specific percentage of the trust assets are paid each year.

The second payment type is a grantor trust. In this case, a tax deduction is taken immediately for the present value of the stream of payments that will be made to the social enterprise beneficiary. This calculation is complicated by different tax treatments, depending on whether the beneficiary is a public charity or a foundation. The trust's income is not taxed to the donor during the term of the trust.

Charitable Annuity

In this case, the social enterprise receives outright title to the assets, and a nonvariable set of annuity payments is sent to the donor (until his death or the death of both spouses).

1. This approach allows the donor to take an immediate tax deduction, which is actuarially determined and is a function of the donor's age and income stream (usually around 10–50% of the face value of a policy, depending on the age of the donor or donors). For an 81-year-old male (with a 78-year-old spouse), for example, a $100,000 gift would produce an immediate $37,000 tax deduction.

2. If the gift is made in appreciated securities, the donor avoids the potential capital gains tax on the appreciation part of the

securities. The $100,000 is now outside the donor's estate and is thus eliminated from all federal, state, and local inheritance taxes.

3. A fixed stream of annuity payments (in this case of $6,513/year) is made each year (usually quarterly) for the lives of the two annuitants. This stream is considered taxable income to the annuitants.

4. For public recognition purposes, most development departments treat this as a $100,000 gift, the same as if it were in cash (it is, of course, worth substantially less to the social enterprise because they only get to use all the money when both annuitants have passed). This vehicle together with its treatment is actively promoted by most development organizations only to individuals in their late 70s and beyond. The tool is designed to provide income security to the donor and a gift of a certain amount to the social enterprise.

5. Roughly half the assets are immediately available to the social enterprise and the remainder at the end of the annuity. As noted earlier, all assets in this vehicle have been completely removed from the estate of the donor and thus are not subject to inheritance taxes.

Donor-Advised Fund

This is a flexible way to give to social enterprise. The donor can choose which years to make a charitable deductible gift and at that time put the money in a donor-advised fund. The donor, however, can spread the actual payments from the donor advised fund to social enterprises over a number of years. A donor-advised fund's financial assets are managed both for logistical and investment purposes by a money manager. The fund gives the donors great flexibility in the type of assets the donor can give. The mechanics of a donor-advised fund are as follows:

1. The donor gives assets to the fund and gets an immediate tax deduction. These assets can include normal items such as cash and publicly funded securities, but also items such as bit coins, private equity interests, and so forth.
2. A money manager handles the assets until they are distributed to a social enterprise. Any appreciation that occurs in the assets while they are in the fund is completely tax free. The money manager handles all the recordkeeping.
3. The donor gets to decide when to distribute the assets and to which social enterprises.
4. This fund is strictly for social enterprise purposes.

Foundations

The tools and techniques in this chapter have so far focused on mechanisms focused on individual giving. These ranged from the straightforward cash gift to the charitable remainder trusts. In aggregate, if one combines individual giving and bequests, $352 billion of total US philanthropy of $450 billion in 2019 came from individuals or 78% of the total. Where did the rest come from? Overwhelmingly, from foundations who contributed $76 billion or 17% of total philanthropy. Corporations at $21 billion (5% of the total) comprised the rest. Who are these foundations?[1] As of March 2020, foundations held nearly $1.0 trillion of assets.[2]

These foundations range from the very small (a few $100,000 of assets) to the top 100 foundations whose assets range from $400 million to nearly $49 billion.

A foundation can be an intermediate step to begin the process of promulgating a multigenerational legacy of philanthropy beyond the tools described in this chapter. Its creation requires substantial

---

[1]*Giving USA*, June 16, 2020.
[2]Board of Governors of the Federal Reserve System, June 11, 2020.

tax and legal inputs to come up with an appropriate governance structure. Each foundation is highly customized to the needs and wishes of a particular donor. There is not a generic prototype. Key aspects of a foundation include the following:

1. A donor's contributions to the foundation in any year can be up to 30% of adjusted gross income for cash and 20% for long-term publicly traded securities. These numbers have varied over the years and will almost surely change as administrations in Washington change. Contributions may be cash, stock, real estate, and so forth.
2. There is no federal tax on the investment income of the foundation. There is, however, an excise tax of 1–2%. Additionally, at least 5% of the assets must be distributed to social enterprises of the donor's choice each year.
3. Either a relative of the donor or a professional may perform management tasks of the foundation.

The hammering out of the foundation's mission statement and its investment priorities can start important (never before had) discussions about the donor's values. Often, both the different generations of the donors and specific individuals may have very different priorities, which may be both intense and deeply held. Over time, new priorities often form and the mission statement requires changes.

As the following paragraphs show, foundations have played an important role in philanthropic support of social enterprises for a long period of time. A history of a foundation can range from very short (one year) on the one hand to as long as a century, for foundations like the Rockefeller Foundation. As noted later, each has its own unique mission. The great challenge for a social enterprise is sorting out which ones have missions that match to a specific social enterprise's needs and are worth approaching for support via grants. Many foundations wish to support only financially stable organizations, and insist on positive operating cash flow as a condition of making a grant. This can mean at a social enterprise's hour of greatest need, it may be ineligible for support from several foundations that might otherwise have been interested in it because of its mission. Repeatedly, the author has been in situations where his organization has been on the short end of these requests. A large foundation was hoped to be the social enterprise's lifeline to the future until suddenly the enterprise was discovered to be ineligible for a grant because of the very financial weakness it was hoping to address with the foundation's help.

Foundations have very different missions and ambitions that influence their grant-making ability. Consider three very different major foundations with widely varying missions. First is the Bill and Melinda Gates Foundation. Created in 2000, as of December 31, 2018, it had $46.8 billion of assets and a global staff of nearly 1,500 employees. Its stated mission is "To work to help all people lead healthy and productive lives. In developing countries, it focuses on improving people's health and giving them the chance to lift themselves out of hunger and extreme poverty. In the United States it seeks to ensure that all people, especially those with the fewest resources, have access to the opportunities they need to succeed in school and life."[3]

To deliver on this mission, the organization's grant-making activities are broken into five programs—namely, (1) global development, (2) global growth and opportunity, (3) global health, (4) global policy and advocacy, and (5) the United States. Its office includes New Delhi, Beijing, Lagos, Johannesburg, London, Washington, and Seattle. Known for the same tight management control as its originator, Microsoft, its impact has been immense. It brings to the organizations they help not just money, but also, as importantly, competence, contacts, and focus. Large, high-impact societal projects are its target. Like its founders, the foundation is

---

[3]Wikipedia, August 10, 2020.

looking for transformational impact on the major problems of our time—for example, the elimination of malaria.

A very different organization, located on the opposite coast of the North American continent, is the over-100-year-old Rockefeller Foundation. Founded in 1913, with resources from the breakup of Standard Oil, it is one of the longest-standing foundations in the United States. The 39th largest foundation in the United States, in 2017 it had assets of $4.1 billion. Among its many achievements over a century was enabling the establishment of the John Hopkins School of Public Health, Harvard University's School of Public Health, and the invention of the yellow fever vaccine. Today the Foundation is focused on four core commitments—namely, to end energy poverty, achieve health for all, nourish the world, and expand economic opportunity. It tries to do this through innovative partnerships and impact investments. Most recently, it has been investing on the forefront of the Coronavirus Covid-19 crisis. Spending at an annual rate of $173 million (as of 2016), it operates globally with offices in Washington, DC, Nairobi, Bellagio, Italy, in addition to its New York headquarters. Like the Gates Foundation, it focuses on mega problems constrained, of course, by being one-tenth its size.

Formed more recently is the Boston-based Barr Foundation. Founded in 1999, and 62nd in asset size in the United States, it has given over $1 billion in grants since its founding. It gave $90 million of grants in 2019 and had $1.8 billion of assets as of December 31, 2018. Its mission as communicated in its website is threefold: (1) elevating the arts and enabling creative expression, (2) advancing solutions in clean energy, mobility, and climate resilience, (3) helping more young people succeed in learning, work, and life. It has a strong regional focus.

It responded generously and immediately to the 2020 Coronavirus Covid-19 crisis with nearly $6 million of grants in April–July 2020 to Massachusetts organizations, including Massachusetts Community Foundations, immigrant-serving organizations, and organizations serving black communities. Its work has a very specific regional focus. Like the other two organizations, it has retained strong management and has a laser focus on its priorities.

Understanding the ecosystem of these foundation resources is where a well-connected trustee can make a major contribution. Knowing of their existence and having the ability to pick up a telephone and establish an initial contact for the social enterprise is invaluable. To make this work, the social enterprise needs one or more individuals who know how to write grant proposals that resonate with the target.

In some cases (small organizations), a board member may be the grant writer. The author recently received an email from the president of a small museum that noted, in part, "All projects, equipment or programs that require expenses are grant funded. One of our board members is an experienced grant writer, so with our mission and 'scrappy' way of getting things done, we do pretty well with grants. What has really allowed us to grow (and get our buildings in better shape), has been two $100,000 grants from XYZ foundation ($50,000/year half for preservation and half for youth education). We are currently in the final year of XYZ foundation funding and are hoping they will invest in us again." This story captures both the upside of foundation funding and its risks, namely:

1. Preparing a proposal is time consuming and the likelihood of success under best circumstance is somewhat below 100%. There is a real premium on uncovering and targeting the foundations most relevant to a social enterprise's individual situation before spending significant resources on a grant proposal.
2. A social enterprise looks for stability in the income stream. In this context, repetitive gifts are highly desirable. Conversely, many foundations like to get things started and then move on to other projects, leaving the social enterprise with a financial hole to fill. Even worse is when the social enterprise has

built up its expenses to improve its service reach and suddenly the foundation moves on. As a result, the social enterprise may wind up in a worse financial position than if they had never started down this path.

Summary

There is a wide variety of tools to help execute a donor's planned giving strategy, which, intelligently applied, can effectively support both their heirs and the causes they are interested in, while minimizing their tax burden. The establishment of a planned giving program requires a lot of thinking at the beginning by the donor. Additionally, as one ages, one's priorities may change, and changes will likely be necessary. Some planned giving tools are irrevocable, whereas others are not. Also both the social enterprises that donors are interested in and the best ways to support them continue to evolve as donor interests, social enterprise needs, and laws change. The material in this chapter is necessarily suggestive in nature. Execution requires close work with both lawyers and financial planners to get the best result for individual situations. For the social enterprise, on the other hand, planned giving is a vital tool to allow it to participate in the current intergenerational transfer of wealth that is occurring. The benefits can greatly outweigh the complexities of getting started.

Foundations represent an important source of financial support for social enterprise. Appropriately uncovering their existence and accessing their support require both knowledgeable staff and well-connected trustees to identify the ones who could be potentially interested in supporting the social enterprise's mission. Access to strong grant-writing skills and relationship management are key to bringing them into the fold as active supporters. Once in the fold, keeping them there requires both effort and creativity. The right trustee can be so helpful here.

Questions a trustee should ask about planned giving
and foundations

- Do we have a trained planned giving officer who can explain planned giving instruments and facilitate their use?
- Who is managing our planned giving assets? Do they have experience and credibility?
- Does our organization have sufficient potential planned giving donors to warrant investment in this capability?
- If our organization is of a subcritical mass to offer this capability on an ongoing basis, can we create a strategic alliance with someone who has these capabilities?
- Can I identify and help access potential foundations that could help support us?
- Does our organization have skilled grant writers? If not, can we get access to them when needed?
- Can we identify potential trustees who could help us with grant preparation and foundation access?

7

Events

HUMAN BEINGS FOR the most part are naturally socially gregarious animals. When you appropriately involve and engage them in social activity, they are capable of rising to great philanthropic generosity. Consequently, no discussion of philanthropy can ignore the subject of meaningful tasteful events as part of a successful development strategy. Participation in tasteful events can quicken one's enthusiasm for an organization's mission, performance, and its projects. This chapter discusses a taxonomy of development events that are offered in the normal course of time in social enterprise organizations with examples of where and how they have been successful.

I will start with a few generalizations about what the hallmarks of a good event are in general, and then dive into a taxonomy of the various events a social enterprise might offer during a year.

What are the general characteristics of a successful event?

- It is engaging and entertaining in format. New material about the organization and its plans is tastefully presented with appropriate use of graphic and video aids. Intense interactive give and take during the event with the group's members is usually critical as well. People tend to feel warmer about the value added of the projects, the more they have time to discuss and ask questions about the projects. Incorporating this feedback in the next iteration of the project often both improves the project and expands its support. Over time, however, formats become tired, and various types of new events need to be offered, even if the old ones were very financially successful.

- The event and its accomplishments are clear in the audience's mind a week after it occurs. This is particularly important if new individuals were being exposed to these messages for the first time.
- Appropriate background materials are provided as takeaways to reinforce the message. These include brochures, copies of PowerPoints, video streams, and so forth.
- A critical mass of the right individuals for this event is assembled (always meet in a room slightly too small). (The crowdedness adds ambiance and gives the feel of an unexpected success, which helps positively shape the dialogue's tone.) The right people feed off each other's energy.
- The physical environment is appropriate for the event and tasteful for the type of organization making this type of presentation (neither too lavish nor too sparse).
- Next steps to be taken by the organization and meeting attendees are both seen as welcome and clear to all who attended the event.
- New advocates for the organization and its projects were surfaced.

The following paragraphs identify typical events offered by social enterprises in the course of a year and some cautionary notes about them.

Board Events

Although the board is responsible for both the governance of the organization and, particularly in the context of this book, for fundraising, it is also a social organization. In this context, how it spends its time together is very important to help deepen commitment of its members to the organization and encourage their self-solicitation.

The following points are critical:

Time together is essential

- The time together must be long enough for the board members to get to know each other. Three two-hour meetings in the course of a year are not enough for this purpose. Resulting lack of board connectedness can lead to real problems in a crisis. Board meeting efficiency is not necessarily always desirable. Effectiveness is a better measure. An annual offsite retreat is a very appropriate way to facilitate these social interactions. Such a retreat needs to be organized in a way that there is opportunity for substantial member-to-member interaction with contributions being made by most, if not all, members. It should take place in a location with appropriate ambiance for the type of organization it is (the Four Seasons Hotel is not the right place for a church vestry retreat). The informal linkages forged in these retreats can foster unexpected collaborations. For example, the author recalls a museum board offsite several years ago that began with a cocktail party at a trustee's house, whom the author barely knew beforehand. It was a very pleasant occasion with good chemistry arising between the two trustees. Six months later, the host called the author to see if he would be willing to be a paid sponsor for a regional museum gala event that was being organized by this trustee. It was very easy for the author to say yes, to this, plus, as it turned out, for the next two annual galas in this location as well. Relationships inside the board really matter in so many ways.

Scheduled board meals are important

- Regular board meetings often end with a reception or dinner with key staff and professional people. These informal conversations form the basis of relationships, which can lead to sensible conversations as future challenges and opportunities emerge for the organization. In fact, more good work is often done in these pre- and postmeeting discussions than in the meeting itself.

Board corporation/overseer events are important

- A joint cocktail party dinner with the corporators/overseers to ensure the board knows the individuals in that group and thus helps bind them more closely to the organization.

Unscheduled time is important

- Unscheduled free time before and after a meeting with coffee or a drink allows important offline discussions to occur and to build relationships. I always add extra time in my schedule to allow the space for this to happen.

The interplay of all of this was vividly captured by an arts organization of a board the author studied several years ago. It used to meet four times a year for 1.5-hour highly efficient meetings. The reality was that new board members, after 1.5 years of service, still did not know all other members by name, let alone anything about their interests. It was easy to skip meetings if scheduling conflicts emerged because the meeting did not seem to add much value. Lengthening the meetings to three hours (with meaningful periods of discussion on important issues) plus an annual day-and-a-half offsite visit completely transformed the board processes in terms of amount and quality of their discussions, attendance, their personal comfort with each other, and ultimately their individual philanthropy. (Most spouses accompanied the group for the annual retreat. This joint activity as a couple dramatically changed the philanthropic contributions of several members because contributions to the organization came to be seen by the family as a joint gift of the couple to an organization that both now understood.) The retreats were balanced to include visits to both well-performing and poor-performing sites, helping the board members better understand the issues facing the organization. As such, the organization became real in the eyes of its trustees who were much more able to internalize its strengths and weaknesses. Years later in board meetings, references would come up about sites visited in the past.

Annual Events

In the course of a year, a series of events takes place that must be planned and delivered on. These events may be few or numerous in number, depending on the context. In no particular order, these events can include the following:

- Opening and closing events for the annual fund. At a church, for example, short presentations on the annual fund, its goal, and its success are made around two luncheons to which all parishioners are invited. The first luncheon introduces the annual fund and asks for support. The second luncheon celebrates the campaign's success (these events are buttressed, of course, by written and mailed materials to both old parishioners and new parishioners). Both long-term parishioners and new parishioners attend these meetings.
- Targeted events for specific subsets of potential supporters. A school studied, for example, holds periodic events throughout the year for alumni; for younger alumni, these are beer and pizza events at a local bar. Connectivity to alumni in the early years after their graduation turns out to make a huge difference in their philanthropy in later years as their personal finances improve.

  For older alums, the school holds a series of briefing cocktail party receptions in major cities where the head is often the key speaker. There is also an annual alumni day on campus for all alums. Most important, however, are the every-five-year alumni events for classes on the occasion of their 5th, 10th, etc., reunions. As noted in Chapter 4, these reunions have both a substantive social/education component and a fundraising component. Different alums and staff are responsible for each component but there is close coordination (great reunion events help create very positive feelings in alums about the institution, which substantially help the fundraisers).

The planning of an alumni events schedule, of course, has to be very age-specific. A 30th reunion, for example, can handle a great deal of walking and stand-up cocktail parties. A 60th reunion, however, must involve a lot more sitting down and not so much walking (30-year-old planners for these events have to remember they are planning events for 80-year-olds with canes, walkers, etc.). In a similar vein, nighttime events that involved driving after dark are not usually seen as good ideas for the older reunions, so venues for their events have to be thought about differently for the older classes than the younger ones.

- Organizations that have introduced planned giving programs normally create a society to which all their donors belong. These societies usually have annual and semi-annual meetings with meals and a speaker. The subtext of these warm gatherings is to make sure people do not undo their legacies and also to stimulate additional planned gifts. These legacy society meetings can turn out to be very profitable with many planned gifts flowing directly from them. Discussion on the performance of your past gifts with a major gifts officer leads naturally to discussion of future ones you might make.

- Schools and colleges often have alumni clubs all around the United States and the globe. A very popular convening mechanism for a club is for the club to host an annual dinner to honor a local alum or local leader and present the individual with a "business statesman of the year" award. The proceeds from this dinner then go to fund scholarships at the institution or some other worthwhile purpose.

- Graduation events are a critical component of school and college life. Not only do they give a lifetime of memories (for parents in particular), but they are important fundraising occasions for class gifts from both parents and the members of the graduating class.
- For museums, schools, and colleges, there are regularly scheduled events throughout the year to which donors at a certain giving level are invited to attend. At a local museum, for example, curators regularly run special tours or presentations preceded by hors d'oeuvres. These events combine high intellectual content with social connectivity to help bind friends closer to the institution and thereby increase their support.
- Organizations arrange special exhibitions or speaker series. Early entry to these exhibitions and invitations to dine with the speaker can be arranged for major donors (these events are often targeted at high-end giving levels such as platinum, gold, or silver).
- Additionally, special speakers may be selected to be honored for their contribution to a field of relevance to the social enterprise. Attendance at these events can be restricted to donors of a certain level or higher. Alternatively, such an event is used as a fundraiser. Several of the social service agencies in Boston, for example, do this.
- Retirement of key leaders (lay or trustee) is an opportunity for an event around the announcement of a creation of a special endowment fund or special naming opportunity in honor of the individual. Such events, of course, have honorary chairs and vice chairs, who are important supporters of these events.

Special Events

For some organizations, a critical part of their financial profiles are funds from special events. A few examples will give you a feeling of the breadth of these activities.

Gore Place is a house museum in the suburbs of Boston with a beautiful former governor's house, a barn remodeled to be suitable for conferences, and a working farm. A major piece of its funds comes from an annual one-day sheep shearing festival, complete with food stands and a Ferris wheel. On a beautiful late April Saturday, a crowd of 7,000–10,000 will arrive and spend lavishly. Conversely, on a cold rainy Saturday in April, only 2,000 may come. You can visualize the stress on the board and management of this organization when a piece of the entire year's financial success depends on a good weather day in late April in New England. Additional funds, of course, come from a string of weddings, plus Christmas and spring galas for friends.

A second example is a large K–12 day school that has a very large parent's association. The parent's association supports every athletic team with drinks and sandwiches for every home game. The head, trustees, and senior leadership regularly attend these games because it is an excellent way to meet parents who potentially can be turned into supportive board members. The author clearly remembers being recruited by a school head off the sideline of a soccer game his 10th-grade daughter was playing in. He ultimately spent 11 years on the board, chairing it for 5 years. Traditionally at this day school, the parent's association each year runs a parents day, built around athletic contests and a big parent dinner with both a silent auction and a public auction. The day raises over $100,000.

A third example is a major hospital that has a three-legged development strategy. The legs are an annual fund, a large gala each year, and a five-year capital campaign. The gala nets over $500,000 through a combination of vendor sponsorships, other event sponsors, over 500 attendees, plus a silent and a public auction. The hospital's major vendors are all supporters of the gala, as are all trustees. A fourth (but more minor leg) is the hospital's annual golf tournament (the CEO is a very good golfer with her handicap being low single digits).

A final example is a major museum that conducts several galas each year in different regions as major fundraisers to complement its annual fund. Either honoring some individual or celebrating an acquisition, an organizing committee is assembled each year for each of these galas to recruit an appropriate set of sponsors and attendees. These are board-sponsored activities. It is expected that each board member will support at least one of the galas each year as a significant sponsor. In addition, they offer a series of special parties and fund-establishing events to honor key retiring members of staff and trustees. In general, they work to ensure that no significant event will go untestimonialized.

Ancillary uses of facilities are an important class of fundraising events for some organizations. We have already talked about using a site owned by the social enterprise for weddings or a board retreat. For school and universities, a big opportunity is the use of athletic fields for summer camp and sports programs or classrooms for special focused courses on science, and so forth. One needs to be sure that the fees from these uses will be enough to cover the wear and tear on the facilities (a temptation is to underprice these programs by ignoring these costs). These uses can also provide additional summer employment for the organization's regular staff, which can bind them closer to you.

Trips

A popular fundraiser with high-upside development potential is a trip organized by the social enterprise to an interesting, often distant, site accompanied by a curator and/or the CEO. The author has been on 10-day church-sponsored trips to the Holy Land and to cathedrals in Europe. He has also been on ones to museums and historic homes, both domestic and abroad, which have lasted from 3 days to a week. On the negative side, these trips can be enormously consuming of the organization's resources with the direct financial contribution to the social enterprise of the trip being very small, relative to the effort to organize it. If, conversely, you look at the trip as a high-end relationship-building mechanism with key potential donors, that allows you to think about it in an entirely different way. Gathering the right donors, trustees, and CEO on a trip can build lasting commitments and relationships, which can really benefit the organization with buildings, scholarships, and endowed position in the future.

A particularly successful one was a three-week trip to China, organized by one of the author's university colleagues. On the trip was the vice-chair of the corporation (the university's governing body), his wife, and some 12 other distinguished graduates. Looking at the output of the trip, five years later, it could be said to include a named professorship for the colleague, the addition of significant research funds to the university, and lifelong personal and professional relationships between the members of the trip and the faculty member, leading to a steady flow of reunion funds. Of course, it does not always work out that way.

A museum's CEO as a matter of policy always tries to go on his organization's high-end donor trips. This, of course, is enormously time consuming. This in turn puts tremendous pressure on him and the development organization to get the right people on the trip. For a museum CEO, spending high-quality time with major donors visiting complementary sites of relevance to the museum is a dream come true. There are, of course, many other reasons for trips. For example:

A major nonprofit educational institution wanted to significantly internationalize its faculty. They came up with the idea of running a global alumni conference of 500–700 people every two years in places like Hong Kong, Shanghai, Cape Town, Frankfurt, and Buenos Aires to force international involvement. In advance of each conference, key faculty did research work in the relevant geographic area. They met in advance local CEOs, some of whom subsequently made presentations at the conference. The conferences, costly to deliver, were a great success for deepening international connectedness for the faculty who had their research agendas reshaped in surprising and significant ways.

Capital Campaigns

Capital campaigns are very event intensive. The following examples are illustrative of typical events:

Small-group scoping events. These are usually groups of potential major supporters, chaired by the CEO who is simultaneously learning, shaping, and selling his priorities. They are very much two-way dialogues. Over the course of the scoping events, patterns can emerge that are quite surprising to the CEO. For example, several years ago, a school had a strategic plan that had a theater as one of its centerpieces. The head was sure the school's supporters who were attending these events would see it as necessary. Twenty supporter events later, she realized that not one of them had reaffirmed the importance of the theater. It was subsequently dropped and replaced by a student center. The scoping events are vital in teasing out priorities.

Preparation of major prospects for silent-phase gifts. Organized by the campaign steering committee, these events may be given not just in the city where the organization's headquarters is domiciled, but around the country and even in overseas capitals like London and Hong Kong, where potential supporters may be located. To be successful, these events require the right combination of investment ideas with a carefully curated list of potential donors. A major K–12 school did two of these events three years apart around major construction projects. Hosted by a parent trustee, 35 couples, the school head, the architect, the head of development, and half the board were at each meeting. Both events presented the building projects as board approved and personally supported projects. The vision and enthusiasm coming from these meetings set the backdrop for a series of separate meetings between the head, the development director, and the individual families over the next several months, where the specific ask for support was made. The host trustee picked up the expense for each event, which is not an unusual occurrence.

Public-phase launch events. These events celebrate the success of the silent-phase part of the campaign. They are also aimed at bringing in the next phase donors, who, in aggregate, tend not to be as affluent as those in the silent phase meetings described earlier. These events are much larger in terms of number of attendees. The speakers are as good but the per capita out-of-pocket expenses tend to be lower as the entire event is less glitzy.

Campaign close events. Scheduled to thank major contributors to date, they also turn out to be new-friend-attracting events. They also establish useful deadlines for late donors and repeat donors from other campaigns. When one of these individuals sees that you personally have given, it is a very powerful motivator for them to join in. Again, the character of the organization impacts the type of venue that is appropriate for the event.

An interesting footnote is the observation that events hosted by supporters in their homes are especially effective. Not only do the guests enjoy the unusual home ambiance, but it is a great source of satisfaction to the host because she/he gets to display his or her house. It is odd but true that giving a $10,000 party may motivate you to give an extra $500,000 gift.

Summary

Event planning is a specialty of the development department. The department must have great creativity and be able to conceive of events appropriate to the specific constituencies and the type of organization they are embedded in. A pizza party for the students, for example, may be the best support for a school hockey game. Conversely, a museum or symphony event for sponsors might best be a black tie evening with a choral or musical accompaniment. The conclusion of a diocesan campaign was a beer and wine reception in an elegant club with hors d'oeuvres for 200 clergy and major donors. These are not cookie-cutter occasions, but require considerable crafting to deliver the right ambiance. Furthermore, the format of these events must be refreshed over time. The annual gala can suddenly seem shop worn. You may have to try something less financially remunerative at the beginning to get a new concept going.

A final irreverent note. When you are having fun, your philanthropic juices tend to run deeper. Some of the great fundraising events in the author's life involved laughing so hard at some outrageously appropriate comment that he could scarcely hold the pen to write a check.

Questions a trustee should ask about events

- Do we have appropriate events for all critical constituencies? Are there addressable gaps?
- Are we evaluating payoff from these events? Are we clear why each one is being done? These can be expensive in terms of time and money.
- Are our events fresh or do they have a tired timeworn feel to them?
- Do we have a process, after several years of doing an event, to review its effectiveness?
- Is participation in these events the best possible use of our CEO's time? Do they highlight her strengths?
- Are our events forward-looking and reaching to customers and donors of the future?
- Are there particular events that I can usefully support by my involvement, financial capability, connections, and so forth?

8

Information Support

A READER OF a decade ago could pick up a copy of this book and find the subject matter of the previous chapters to be familiar. The mechanisms of the annual fund, capital campaign, planned giving and events have remained basically intact. Not so with information support, communications, and operational activities. The very fabric of those activities has been ripped apart and totally redefined by technology. Only the final mechanism of the donor ask either face-to-face, via ZOOM[1] or via telephone remains intact. Awareness raising, education, and brand building activities, however, have been transformed beyond recognition. The great challenge today is how to adapt these new technology vehicles to reach the new generation of younger donors, while not losing contact inadvertently with older donors. Of course, some new technologies like ZOOM are so simple they have even achieved remarkable penetration with the older generation. I recently observed a ZOOM-enabled 65th high school reunion of 20 people all over 80 years old. It was a lively, highly interactive, and spontaneous discussion, which vividly showed how the combination of high-speed bandwidth and cheap high-resolution digital graphics have changed the world of communications for all age cohorts

---

[1]ZOOM, a product of a Nasdaq company, is the leader in video conferencing using the Internet.

(the session also facilitated three alumni gifts, each a $100,000 charitable annuity).

In short, the information revolution has totally transformed both the process of donor identification and the subsequent building of donor awareness of the organization's needs. Several forces have collided which, in the process of allowing the building of some of the most valuable publically traded companies in the world, have also transformed development activities of organizations of all sizes (see Exhibit 8.1 for the eight most valuable publically traded companies in 2020, of which seven are technology companies with all but one of these being information services providers).

How did this happen?

First, the transformation has been driven by the explosion of the availability of very high-speed, very cheap, optical fiber cable and wireless (produced by Cisco and the Chinese manufacturer Huawei, among others). High-resolution digital video content is now delivered almost costlessly to PCs, tablets, and handheld devices for presentation purposes via this new channel. It turns out that today's interactive video conversations are now as easy to initiate and conduct at a lower cost than the long-distance audio telephone conversations of a generation ago. The second component of the transformation is the chip-enabled revolution. Intel (the leading US chip manufacturer, which had a $247 billion market cap as of July 1, 2020) created chips that enabled the emergence of inexpensive, computationally powerful, color graphic handheld devices like iPhones for end users (every development officer now has one). The final step in the transformation was in central offices and cloud farms (think Amazon). These are large-capacity data-processing devices with powerful social media software provided by Facebook, Instagram, Google, Twitter, Oracle, and so forth. The combination of those three items very rapidly resulted in development becoming a capital-intensive electronic-information-supported activity. In embracing these tools, development organizations have totally transformed their operational, prospecting, and other marketing activities.

The key elements of this transformation are described in more detail later. In aggregate, they represent a true revolution. Not that long ago, the tools used by the development department to communicate the organization's products and services that needed funding were primarily paper oriented. They were comprised of colorful annual reports, project brochures, nicely packaged individual stewardship reports, and so on. For capital campaigns, movies and videos were often prepared as well. Today, if these documents and films even exist, they are found only at the periphery, mostly for use by older people who still feel more comfortable with physical documents in their hands. The timing and ease of explaining the financial impact of different donation strategies to potential donors has been revolutionized. As will be discussed in Chapter 9, this impacts the micro social enterprise as much as the medium-sized or gigantic organization.

Website

At the center of today's electronically presented organization is the website. The website lays out in great detail an overview of the organization as well as descriptions of the organization's products and services. These websites normally include welcoming text or video comments by the CEO and the chair (pictures and video are used as well for these messages). The website contains an easily accessible potpourri of text, photography, and videos. In totality these items highlight the key aspects of the organization's operations, services, and the multiple ways donors can support it. The website is usually designed and installed by outside consultants and technicians, who are specialists in mobilizing the relevant technologies. Key aspects of a good website include the following:

- Having a modern up-to-date feel to it. As the world and the organization change, the website's content and format must also change to reflect both new priorities of the organization and the new technical capabilities of websites. All too often, the word *tired* is used to describe an existing website. Continual updates, plus every two years or so a complete reconceptualization, must take place. Technology evolves and industry standards for presentations rise continually. All this will be designed by teams, most of whose members are barely out of their teens.

- High-impact presentations and ease of navigation to key pieces of data are hallmarks of a successful website. Effective use of color, video, and graphics permeate every aspect of this endeavor. Fast response time and an intuitive menu are other critical aspects of a well-designed website.

- Ease of maintenance and updating of the website are critical. It must be easy for staff to plug in, on a continuous basis, updated schedules of events, meetings, and so forth. It is the central hub of the organization and provides the critical links and highways to users accessing its services.

- Passwords and other security measures are critical. Exposure to hacking is an ever present danger, and today's hackers are ever more sophisticated. You need to be easily accessible but also safe. Part of the website should be available to the world, other parts available only for insiders, and still other parts only for selected groups of insiders such as trustees, customers, and alumni relations people.

- Upgrades are often very painful and disruptive to users. Wherever I travel today, most often the organization's master website seems to be in the process of being upgraded, with major service interruptions and delays a matter of course.

- Rapidly expanding capability and access to ever-more-sophisticated information content. For example, some websites now carry drone flyovers of building and campus layouts. You can easily do 3D walking tours of building interiors, seeing lab layouts, and so forth. This, as described later, is all easily downloaded to a laptop or tablet for use in one-on-one potential donor presentations.

- Uptime is critical, with good practice now being over 99% availability.

The website is literally the front door to your organization. Consequently, it must be user friendly, informative, and have very fast response time. It goes without saying, of course, its content must be accurate and up to date. Customized versions are normally prepared for Facebook and other platforms. These websites must be synchronized whenever they are updated.

Communications

High-speed connectivity is the watchword of the twenty-first century. The standard of excellence has changed dramatically in this domain. In the post-Coronavirus Covid-19 world, the web-based software package ZOOM has become the overnight global de facto standard of excellence for donor solicitor meetings (other competitors are Cisco's Webex and Microsoft's Teams packages). In a very short period of time, this capability has driven the landline telephone into further obsolescence. ZOOM at the moment is the global standard with very high fidelity in picture, audio, and supporting materials. In the last month, uses of it by the author have included the following:

- Multiple online training sessions of 30–100 people with intense two- and three-way dialogue occurring.
- Committee meetings of 10–15 people with high interactivity and multiple documents being shared by the different participants.
- Attendance at lectures of 100 or more people with interactive questions at the end.
- Attendance at a half-dozen large graduation and convocation events, which would have been logistically complex to attend in person. Physical attendance, of course, would have violated completely any efforts to appropriately do social distancing.
- Receipt of a warm, personalized one-minute thank-you video from the CEO of an organization to which I had just made a personal gift. It was a high-impact and personalized message, and I found myself, after viewing it, wishing I had given more.

The ZOOM platform easily allows the sharing of multiple slide decks and videos. Afterwards, these items can be put into prospective donors' hands in either written or electronic form. A warning! As you enter the world of ZOOM communications, conferences that combine some people on video and others only on audio can lead to very misleading exchanges. For example, the people who saw the 1960 presidential debate between Kennedy and Nixon on TV came to a very different conclusion about the winner as opposed to those who heard it on radio. Substantial miscommunication can occur if part of the group has visual cues to go along with speech, while the other part of the group misses all the visual information. This can be critical if the subjects being covered are sensitive or emotional. As a result, some organizations now mandate that on their conferences, 100% of the participants must be either on video or else no video capability is allowed.

Looming out of this has been a significant disruption in workspace and the need for individuals to spend 40 hours in the office each week. The second and third quarters of 2020, ravaged by the Coronavirus Covid-19 pandemic, unmistakably showed that large amounts of work could be moved at no diminution of performance from the office to the home, not just on a temporary basis but also on a permanent basis. Some Google employees in California will spend more than a year working from home before returning to the office. The author watched a social enterprise board he is a member of recently triple the amount of time spent in face-to-face meetings. However, because the meetings were all done on ZOOM instead of in person, the commute time to and from a meeting, formerly an hour each way, dropped to zero. As a result, the board's use of the author's time was actually less than before with no discernible diminution of the quality or quantity of the discussion. Trustees are finding less in-person and more ZOOM meetings a much better use of their time. They can do more for the organization. Similarly, this also turns out to be true for a number of development officers. More time in video contact with potential donors and less time in planes and cars traveling to meet them. Occasional face-to-face contact is helpful, but not for every meeting.

Looking to the future, I anticipate substantial reductions in the need for physical offices because a high flow of ZOOM meetings will continue to replace physical meetings in a postpandemic world. For most people, it will not be an either all-home or all-office decision but rather carving one's time up between the two in appropriate and creative ways. Of course there will always be some sensitive items that are done better on a face-to-face basis.

The ubiquitousness of these examples is overwhelming. Routine interactive, no glitch, low cost, two-way video communications across multiple platforms is here for the nontechie. It operates in the middle space between telephone calls and in-person visits that can involve significant travel. It is a powerful way to make more high-impact calls on potential donors without the many hours of travel often involved. The released time of a trustee or a major gifts officer can be redeployed to either develop more prospects per person or more effectively deepen relationships with existing prospects. Spending hours in transit either in traffic jams or airport delays is sharply reduced (not good news for the transportation industry. Business travel is not going to be the same.).

Database Management

The new technologies allow orders-of-magnitude more information to be gathered, manipulated, and analyzed on both individuals and groups of individuals. For example, a multi-site museum's new software now tracks every member's and trustee's individual use of the organization's facilities and services through the year. This enables special focused events and promotions for just those individuals most likely to be interested in these specialized offerings. Similarly, in the hospital capital campaign described earlier (see Chapter 5), they now have master records that track every interaction of a patient with the hospital (prescriptions, office visits, any test by a doctor). As a result, the patient at home, the involved physicians, and physician assistants all know what has happened to the patient on a consistent basis. Costing the hospital $100 million to install, this capability and transparency were worth every dollar in terms of enhanced service from a patient's view. From the hospital's view, it came to be seen that it was offering higher and more consistent service levels across the patient base. This is what is happening in development to donor management.

These data-linking capabilities are directly relevant to development in so many ways. Today, as a matter of course, in well-architected systems, records of individual calls and the known activities of major donors and prospects are kept together in interlinked electronic form. This allows better tracking of the emerging interests of a donor. It also allows a new trustee or new major gifts officer to pick up the threads of a relationship as it has evolved over the years and quickly be prepared to move it forward.

At a recently studied school, for example, no one in the development department had been there more than five years. Consequently, there were no deep longitudinal personal relationships between today's development officers and potential donors. Fortunately, the procedures and files designed and installed by their predecessors in the development department had been deep and for the most part accurate. This allowed the old relationships to be picked up by the new officers with much less spillage than would otherwise have been the case.

This type of integrated data allows the knowledgeable crafting of targeted invitation lists for cultivation events. It can also trigger identification of individuals who can give talks at appropriate institution events or who can be hosts at alumni events. Particularly for organizations with long histories, it is easy for significant potential donors to be lost in the cracks and not be used in these relationship-strengthening activities. All this can now be managed in a more comprehensive and holistic way. This is the great contribution that Oracle, SAP, and their ilk have made to development.

Engaging potential supporters as members of a planning committee when one is gearing up for a reunion or launching a capital campaign is often a wonderful way to encourage much deeper personal involvement and self-solicitation. All the time the individual is in the room developing potential names for development calls and participating in discussions, they are also soliciting themselves. Similarly, the act of thinking who is appropriate for a task deepens your own understanding of and often commitment to a project. These new systems help target the right people for these roles.

In the same vein, having to introduce a project leader to a meeting of potential donors forces the introducers to learn more about the project so as to sound knowledgeable in their introduction. In short, the combination of internal data and carefully searching external files via Google can help build richer donor profiles. These profiles help both trustees and development professionals better manage potential donor relationships. Good 2020 development is deeply data driven!!

Handheld Portable Intelligence

The new technologies of the iPhone have allowed a total transformation of what occurs in the prospect's home or office in a development presentation. Instead of paper reports and a structured walk-through, very different, far more interactive scenarios can occur. For example, an initial video presentation of a building project by the development officer can be followed by a customized virtual tour of the inside of the facility. This can be followed by a description of the fundraising to date and a specific ask for the prospect's support. All this in the donor's home or office! Using an iPad with its great colors, long battery life, and access to relevant data across the Internet is how the ask is playing out today for an increasing number of donors. Depending on the user's tolerance for complexity, the presentation can be rich and all encompassing or vastly more general, touching qualitatively only the key highlights of the project. It is the solicitor's call on how to play it. Today's technology allows vast amounts of sophistication in data presentations at the donor interface, if that is what the solicitor thinks is called for.

Changing Donor Contact

Each generation is motivated by different stimuli. The older generation for the most part is still paper oriented. Alumni magazines on paper are good reading for them as they sit in a chair in the evening watching TV. A report of donors by size of gift or by class is something to be browsed through in a time of leisure, hopefully stimulating thoughts of personally being on the more generous side as they see what others have done.

Younger donors are different. They communicate voraciously through Twitter, Instagram, and text messaging. Twitter can pick up the latest rumors. It communicates broadly your latest view on anything to your followers. Similarly, Instagram can bring enormous attention to an issue. For example, in the mid-2020 Black Lives Matter uproar, alumni of some 70 secondary schools and universities in the Northeast United States created Instagram accounts entitled Black Lives@XYZ school. Instantly, alumni and current students began posting deeply unfavorable comments to these accounts based on their personal experiences at the institution. These posts instantaneously brought enormous public and internal pressure on the administration and trustees of these institutions to make change. Many of the institutions subsequently put special committees of the board and groups associated with the institution together to engage the issue. We live in a fast-moving global information world, which has swept up almost all aspects of development operations.

Summary

In short, the ask still remains the central task of development. However, it takes place today in a revolutionarily different information environment, one in which potential donors are shaped by many more different types of electronic information and forces than they were in the past. Development in the information age is simply different! It is a massively capital-intensive activity with communications gear, portable intelligence in iPads, large relational databases, and social-media software packages. Realistically, however, in a world increasingly technology-enabled, large gifts from those more seasoned in years will still often be achieved by the interpersonal strategies of the past.

Exhibit 8.1

July 1, 2020 Eight largest public companies ranked by market cap

Apple	$1,569 billion
Microsoft	$1,564 billion
Amazon	$1,432 billion
Alphabet (Google)	$979 billion
Facebook	$675 billion
Tencent	$620 billion
Alibaba	$435 billion
Berkshire Hathaway*	$432 billion

* Nontech company
Based on closing prices on NYSE
Source: Based on The New York Stock Exchange(NYSE).
Intercontinental Exchange, Inc.

Questions a trustee should ask about information support

- Is a relational database installed that is appropriate for my organization?
- If not, are there plans to review this issue?
- Does our website feel state of the art, or is it an embarrassment?
- Do we know what best information support practices are in our industry?
- Are we using professionals appropriately in the design of the information support activity?
- Have we run a professional information security audit?
- Does our staff feel we are appropriately state of the art?
- Are our professionals young enough to really internalize how to use the latest tools for information support?

9

Micro Social Enterprise Issues

THIS BOOK WAS written primarily to help new trustees assist the development activities of organizations that mostly are over $1 million in revenues, have a defined governance structure, and have a history of several years or more. Some of these organizations, like the Metropolitan Museum of Art, Massachusetts General Hospital, or the Smithsonian Institute, are massive and have a global reputation. Others, of course, are much smaller but play vital roles in their region and community. Below these organizations in size, however, are hundreds of thousands of others, which I will call micro social enterprises. With revenues well below $1 million and often no permanent paid staff, they nonetheless play a vital role in their communities. Their organization, leadership, and fundraising structures and processes, however, are very different in form and formality from those of their larger brethren. The earlier ideas in this book are relevant in spirit to those organizations but not necessarily in form. This chapter focuses on their special characteristics and needs.

Who are these organizations? Three examples described later show their wide diversity in structures and needs. Consider first the Boston Terrier Rescue League of Florida. Its mission is "saving Boston Terriers who are lost, abandoned or surrendered in Florida and the southeast United States, regardless of age, health, or adoptability." Their goal is to nourish each Boston terrier back to emotional and physical health, while providing necessary medical care in an environment that fosters trust and alleviates fear. It has revenues of under $170,000 a year, and has no paid staff. The talents and energies of a board of five hard-working volunteers drive this organization. The board consists of a CEO/CFO, who provides leadership and financial skills, a retired veterinarian whose medical guidance is invaluable, a corporate secretary who handles the myriad of legal issues and other regulatory and bureaucratic details, and two vice presidents, who do a variety of leg work projects, including marketing and managing the logistical issues involved with the transport and health of dogs. Their major marketing activity is based around a website designed and maintained by two skilled Apple technicians who volunteer their time and skills on a moonlighting basis (not surprisingly, maintenance and upgrading activities are a continual hassle). Over 200 dogs are identified, processed, and placed in homes all over Florida each year. More than half the organization's expenses are fees paid to veterinarians for various health issues, including vaccinations, detailed physical exams, and so forth. Living hand to mouth, about half of their revenues come from fees of one sort or another; examples include adoption, medical reimbursement, food, and so forth. The rest comes from philanthropic support. PayPal donation links on its website and Facebook pages are an important source of funding. Special promotions such as birthday honoring on Facebook pages with direct payment links are another. Special payments beyond fees by grateful dog owners are yet a third source of funds. Looking for voluntary payments all the time is one of the key tasks of the five board members.

At the same time, overhead expenses are kept to a minimum. There is, for example, no office with key records being kept in the CEO's home office or in the Cloud. Volunteers and board members are continuously moving dogs from one location to another as needed. These individuals donate their time, cars, gas, and often living space for free. With only a small cash reserve, the real asset of the association is not financial but is the passion and commitment of its volunteer board driven by their love of Boston terriers. This is life at the base of the social enterprise pyramid.

A very different type of micro social enterprise is typified by the Friends of Pleasant Bay. Located at the elbow of Cape Cod, Pleasant Bay is a seven-mile-long tidal estuary. The Friends is an environmental organization located in Chatham, Massachusetts, founded over three decades ago in 1985. Over time, its mission has been steadily sharpened and refined. Today it is "To promote education, research and public awareness of this area as one of critical environmental concern, to preserve open space and retain the visual quality of the area, to preserve the environmental integrity of the Bay's shoreline, to ensure habitat protection and retention of the rich biological diversity and productivity of the Bay, to retain and enhance public access to the shoreline, to preserve natural and historic sites, and to promote awareness of historic Native American culture."[1]

The organization has no full-time or part-time paid staff. It is entirely volunteer-driven with annual expenditures of around $60,000. Half of these expenditures consist of education grants of one form or another, all given to support and sustain various activities dedicated to preserving and improving Pleasant Bay. The remaining expenditures are in categories such as miscellaneous printing, postage, website royalty fees, insurance, and accounting. Some $60,000 of revenues is provided by member donations stimulated by semi-annual appeals. None are especially large.

In addition, The Friends undertake periodic fundraising to support large projects of special interest. Two recent ones are of particular note. The first was the raising of $5 million in conjunction with several conservation trusts to acquire Sipson Island in Pleasant Bay for conservation purposes and nature-trail easements. Sipson was the last privately owned island located in salt water on Cape Cod to pass from private ownership to conservation status. It joined a number of other properties that The Friends of Pleasant Bay has helped

---

[1](Website Friends of Pleasant Bay, December 18, 2020)

move to conservation status over the past 30 years. In future years, a spin-off social enterprise, the Sipson Island Trust, will manage the Island, raise funds to restore its pristine nature, and run education and research projects on it. The second project in 2017–2019 was the raising of over $250,000 for the design, construction, and certification of a solar-powered vessel to serve as a floating classroom on the Bay.

The heart of The Friends of Pleasant Bay is its 21-person board of directors. All have homes in the area and most have long histories with boating and other activities on Pleasant Bay. Their skills range from science to education and nonprofit management. They all have a deep network of long-term personal connections in the area, which helps enormously with fundraising for major capital projects. The board is organized into six standing committees. These are:

1. Executive Committee. They are authorized to act for the full board on time-sensitive issues.
2. Finance Committee. They develop and monitor performance of the annual budget as well as oversee the organization's modest assets.
3. Education and Program Committee. They allocate funds for proposals from schools and other organizations that research various aspects for the use of the Bay.
4. Membership Committee. They are responsible for growth and sustenance of membership.
5. Communications Committee. They prepare the design and content of annual newsletters, brochures, and marketing materials.
6. Governance Committee. They ensure appropriate policies and procedures are in place for the organization.

In addition, there are several ad hoc committees of which the most important are nominating (identification and nominating new trustees), special project fundraising, and the science committee. With the governance structure of a much larger organization and access to a network of deep-pockets funding sources, this little virtual organization packs a punch far beyond its size. In 2020, it is filled with innovation, energy, and vitality. As typified by the Sipson Island project, The Friends have had enormous impact in its region.

A very different micro social enterprise is Lake View Park.[2] Located in a rural northern US community, it was founded in 1876 and contains 390 acres of forestland, sports fields, fishing dock, playground, boat launching, and fishing facilities. Founded for the citizens of the town by its original donor, a town resident, it is supported by the combination of the income from a small endowment and user fees for its various facilities such as tennis courts. A small staff and ground equipment are shared with a local nine-hole golf course. A social enterprise for many years, it was governed by the descendants of the original donor. Although the descendants were mostly dispersed around the country, for many years three or four of them, primarily retired individuals, lived locally and kept the Park going through their active volunteer service.

Governance was simple. The nominating committee selected a board of trustees from among the descendants of the founder. The board met annually at the Park to review the financial results of the previous 12 months, a proposed operating budget for the coming 12 months, and a proposed capital budget (and have a great family reunion highlighted by a picnic in the Park). The Park manager (a full-time employee with great mechanical skills who kept the various pieces of machinery in good shape) initially prepared drafts of the operating and capital budgets. The executive committee, composed mostly of the four local trustees then reviewed these drafts and recommended their approval to the board.

During the "season," the local trustees remained very close to the Park operations. In fact, one would come by every day to pick up

---

[2]Disguised name.

the previous day's cash receipts and deposit them in the bank. Operating problems such as uncollected trash, burned-out lawns, and graffiti—all of which would detract from the customer experience—were immediately obvious and actions were taken to have them corrected on the spot. A portfolio of stocks and bonds of modest size had been left by the founder. A local bank under the oversight of the Park board's investment committee managed it. The revenue from the portfolio combined with fees and prudent control expense produced for many years a balanced budget. The park prospered; the trustees enjoyed their annual meetings and their reunions. The town enjoyed the use of the park, ultimately adding a Little League baseball field on the edge of the park with trustee approval.

Then it all started to go downhill. What happened?

1. As years passed, the trustees became ever more remote cousins and the annual meeting became less of a family reunion event of relatives re-engaging and more of a burden of traveling to meet with people they barely knew.
2. The local trustees grew old and passed. Suddenly there were no trustees left who lived in town. Supervising daily activities became a burden, which was not well handled. Problems were either not uncovered or not addressed. The Park began to look shabby, and the number of visitors began to drop.
3. The yield on the endowment declined. Reduction in capital expenditures was made to balance the budget and as a result the Park became even less attractive. Weeds began to appear everywhere and the lakefront was filled with reeds.
4. No effort from the trustees was made to raise money, nor was it clear that it would have been successful if tried. It was not a philanthropy of choice. Honoring a distant ancestor lost its cachet as generations succeeded generations.
5. The trustees and the governance of the Park began to seem remote from the town. Local resentment began to arise in the town's citizenry and selectmen about inept absentee governance.

In short, the passion and the commitment of the volunteers and governance, so clear in the first two organizations, were no longer present in this organization. Confronted with that reality, the trustees of the Park, after some agonizing, agreed to turn over the management of the park and its assets to the town and local trustees. A local resource was back under local control. Since then it has turned around and now thrives.

What do these stories tell us about life of the micro social enterprise? First, the energy and connectedness of the CEO is absolutely key. The founder CEO and her team must be passionate in their belief about the organization's mission and personally committed to raising the funds for it.

Passion. The leader needs to have great passion for the mission of the organization and be willing to undertake great personal risks in its pursuit. The life of a start-up and a small organization is normally volatile and filled with great ups and downs. In these circumstances, it is the personal commitment of the leader that can inspire donors, volunteers, and staff to join the organization to give generously of their time and treasure to the cause. Charisma and boundless energy are critical. Great things are being done by The Friends. The volunteers work tirelessly at Boston Terrier. None of this energy and commitment was present at Lake View Park at its later stages of family management.

Personal Fundraising Skills. Often only a couple of weeks away from insolvency, the CEOs of those organizations are skilled in being able to personally raise funds. Friends and family are first sources. Neighbors and acquaintances are another source. Cold-call solicitation of individuals of means is still another source. Of particular note are those who have a reputation for philanthropy or known interest in supporting similar types of activities. The ability to relentlessly follow-up leads with emails, letters, and telephone calls is key. When in front of individuals, it is the CEO's passion that usually carries the day. Countless times, the pledge is in reality made to the asker and not the cause.

Perseverance. The ability to make multiple calls until, in a moment of weakness or doubt, the potential target agrees to take the call is vital. A particularly memorable event in a campaign was when the eleventh call to a prospect in a year finally broke through and led to an appointment. In due course, the appointment led to a pledge. In this case, the prospect was known to have resources, had given to similar causes, and persistence was warranted. The Boston Terrier volunteers, like their namesake, are relentless in their search for funds.

Networking Ability. If the prospect does not have the resources or interest, they often have friends who can be helpful. Uncovering the existence of these friends is a real art. The core concept is the notion that everyone is, at most, only six levels of separation from anyone else. Schmoozing plays a very important role in the brainstorming sessions with key individuals to uncover these connections. The longer you talk with someone, the more names of prospects tend to pop up. Intriguingly, often the names that emerge a half hour into a conversation are better than the ones surfaced in the earlier part of the conversation. Even better are the ones you wake up thinking of in the middle of the night (and hopefully remember to write down before going back to sleep). My favorite one was a lawyer/school board colleague, who, after talking for an hour suddenly stopped. In an animated way, he described a friend, another lawyer, who was sole trustee of a small foundation whose mission on reflection aligned exactly with that of the small social enterprise he was raising money for. The friend's generosity through the foundation was extraordinary. Ultimately, he became a trustee of the social enterprise, and he helped pave the way for its emergence from the micro category.

Hustle. These organizations are not 9 a.m. to 5 p.m. ones. They require 24-hours-a-day effort and are utterly absorbing. Sitting in your office, or reading a book, will not get it done for you. The more places you go, the more people you interact with, the more likely you are to make something good happen. Someone you meet in one organization can often help you in another endeavor. Watching my daughter's athletic events in high school introduced me to a whole new set of future friends (parents of her classmates) on the sidelines who became helpful in supporting other quite different organizations in subsequent years. The network can never be too big.

Creativity. Support for organizations can come in many forms other than just cash. Donations of services, hard goods like furniture, free rent, and so on, all can help the small enterprise. Expense avoidance through this type of donation can be as useful as cash. At the beginning, a wooden desk, a telephone, and a passionately delivered presentation on mission may be all you need to get started. It is unfair, but given the choice of an inspiring CEO of an organization with an uninspiring mission, or an inspiring mission with an uninspiring CEO, at start-up time I want the inspiring CEO. That person will almost always breathe new life into the mission and transform it into becoming inspiring.

Vulnerability of One. The micro-organizations are almost always excessively dependent on one key person. Often, all key donor relationships are in her hands. When she is healthy and energetic, the organization prospers and grows. Sometimes, however, either passion ebbs or aging kicks in. Very quickly the organization begins to struggle. One of three things will happen. First, the organization increasingly stumbles, making mistakes in either resource allocation or execution and either fades away or drifts toward bankruptcy. Mortality rates of social enterprises like their corporate brethren are very high. Death can arrive with great suddenness. Second, in other cases, although weak, the organization has enough fundraising and service capabilities to be a desirable acquisition by an organization with a similar or allied mission. In an ideal situation, this can allow the founder CEO to fade out with dignity (or even take over leadership of the new organization). A third option is to find a successor CEO to take over either from within or from outside to try and affect a turnaround. This is hard because so many of the personal relationships of the CEO are often vital to the organization's survival. Unfortunately, however, they are often also very hard to transfer to another individual, particularly from the outside. Conversely, an insider CEO candidate may not have the personality or energy to run the organization alone. So often he or she is a good bureaucrat but simply lacks the magic to credibly solicit for funds. All too often, a good second-in-command in micro-organizations lacks the fire, charisma, and self-confidence of a leader who can lead through asking.

In summary, the skills to run a small start-up social enterprise are quite special and unique. It is why so many ultimately fail. It should be noted that for both of the successful organizations described in this chapter, the CEO was an effective fundraiser. A successful micro-nonprofit CEO is often described as a low-priced beggar (in contrast to major university presidents who are high-priced beggars living in beautiful homes). Always living on the edge, their organizations are often only one payroll away from bankruptcy. Although Boston Terrier and Friends of Pleasant Bay are worlds apart in mission and operation, both excelled in this area.

If the leader is the first thing special about the small nonprofit, the second is *governance*. As both the Boston Terrier and Friends of Pleasant Bay cases show, these organizations can often exist with no full-time employees, but rather with just volunteer staff. It is not uncommon for volunteers to wind up working half time or even much longer. Volunteer burnout as a result is a constant risk. All of a sudden someone you were counting on withdraws and you have an operational hole. It is one reason that one looks to raise money so they can retain paid employees and thus hopefully acquire greater stability. This helps, but you are still vulnerable to operational disruption if that person leaves the organization for whatever reason. Small organizations inordinately depend on key people, their often-scarce skills, and organizational knowhow. When they leave or are ill, important knowledge is gone. Equally important are their missing hands. Good governance can help mitigate this by helping provide discipline to match expenditures to the fundraising.

Governance of small social enterprises can be very sketchy, especially at the beginning. It normally begins with just the CEO. A couple of friends, who have some interest in the mission, are then dragged in by the CEO to help, often because they do not know how to say no. Relatively early, someone with bookkeeping or financial skills is then added as treasurer. A working relationship is worked out with an accountant who prepares monthly, quarterly, and annual reports. At Lake View Park, for years, as noted earlier, a trustee who lived in town every day picked up the cash receipts from the previous day and deposited them in a bank account. Each Friday, the bank gave her the paychecks to be handed to the three or four Park employees. She was a very hands-on trustee. Every week she and two other local trustees walked the Park with its manager, identifying various local maintenance issues which needed addressing. Over the course of a year, a list of building repair, machine replacement, and other potential capital projects were prepared. As described earlier, once a year, the trustees came from around the country to socialize, approve the proposed capital budget, review the overall financials, and approve the operating budget for the coming year. The reality, to use the language introduced earlier in the book, was that the three local trustees were the board, and the trustees were really corporators. This happy state of affairs existed for over 50 years. In due course, as noted earlier, the local trustees moved away, died, or became ill. As governance collapsed, the board was able to transform the Park's governance. It turned its assets, plus the portfolio of stocks and bonds, over to a combination of local trustees and town support. Fortunately, that meant that as the original volunteer support evaporated, new volunteers were found and the operation was able to survive and continue its mission of providing its services to the community. This was a happy resolution for a small organization that, as its volunteer governance structure evaporated, it was able to transition in time to salvage delivery of its mission. It is also worth noting that this was a social enterprise whose revenues came 100% from fees and endowment. Neither the CEO nor trustees felt any compulsion to get or give money. It was not a passion that stirred their philanthropic genes, a factor that contributed to its need for restructuring.

Fundraising must always be near the center of the micro social enterprise's management's mind. The CEO's number one responsibility lies in this area. How it is executed depends on the CEO and the type of operation. For ongoing operations, membership payments by check or a PayPal button on a website or Facebook page are normal practices. These payments are triggered by email and direct mail solicitations. You simply need to keep the engine running and the money will come in.

For more significant donations like the Sipson Island purchase or research boat at the Friends of Pleasant Bay, it is the contacts of the CEO and board members who can uncover hidden interest for the project, which is the key to their success. People on the periphery of an organization may have hidden interests and passions. For example, during an earlier campaign, a donor emerged who 50 years earlier had headed a long-since defunct camp sailing program on Pleasant Bay. Happy memories plus more recent engagement with Bay activities made this long shot solicitation a happy, if unexpected, success. Networking and visibility are key. Personal letters, until guilt finally weighs in and wears the recipient down, also sometimes work. Joining clubs and advisory boards to get into a contact network is a well-known tactic, as are speeches at appropriate events and radio interviews. Articles on mission-related activities are another form of outreach.

When you sign up for a mission as head of a micro social enterprise, you also sign up for this fundraising task. Down at the very base of the social enterprise space is the same need for funds that exist for far larger enterprises. The difference, however, is the rapid consequences of a funding failure. The Museum of Fine Arts in Boston, in the midst of the 2020 Covid-19 problem, announced a loss of $14 million and the permanent loss of over 100 jobs. Painful, but the museum will live for another day. Conversely, for the micro social enterprise with similar results, the almost certain result is a fast trip to oblivion.

Questions a CEO and trustee should ask

- How reliable are my cash sources? What could go wrong?
- How big are my reserves? How long can I survive a cash flow interruption?
- Are there untapped clusters of potential donors available for me?
- Are there potential partners I could team with or merge with?
- Do I have the personality and energy to cold call marketing or build a network? If not, can I find someone to partner with?
- Do I have the stamina and intestinal fortitude for this job?
- Do I believe in the mission passionately enough to take the risks?
- Is the passion still there or is it time to quit or merge?

10

What Can I Do?

THE PREVIOUS CHAPTERS identified the different components of the development activity and the very different approaches used by various organizations to implement them. As described, annual fund activities, capital campaign activities, and planned giving each require different processes of execution. Additionally, each social enterprise sector has its special challenges.

When you are considering joining a social enterprise board or actively supporting its development mission with your time, the first and most fundamental question is, "Do I understand and support its mission?" Implicit in this question is that the social enterprise appears to be viable. There are many worthwhile organizations that, for a variety of reasons, are not independently viable going forward. Just as organizations in the for-profit world fail to adapt to a changing world, so also is this true for social enterprises. Hospitals, schools, universities, arts organizations over time may fail, be forced to merge under disadvantageous terms, have the opportunity to make strategic acquisitions, or reinvent themselves through internal initiatives. Understanding the pressures an organization is under and deciding if you want to spend a part of your life with this organization, its challenges and its mission, is the first decision you must make, given the time and resources you will ultimately have to invest. It must be your passion. No one else can make that decision for you.

Having said this, of course, there is only so much you can learn from a position outside the organization. Consequently, an important task in your first six months as a board member or member of the development team is to validate your incoming assumptions about mission and viability to make sure you fully know what you are investing in. Sometimes it makes sense. Sometimes it does not make sense and you will want to disengage.

There are many reasons for disengagement. For example, the author remembers the second social enterprise board he got involved in. It was an organization very close to his heart, being the adoption agency his two oldest children had come from as babies. As he got more involved, he discovered it was an organization staffed by volunteers at the board level, none of whom had regular employment. Board meetings went from 11:30 a.m. to 2:30 p.m. on a midweek day, not including the commute to a downtown location, thereby killing an entire workday. The time requirements did not work for the author, and he had to withdraw from the board and simply support the organization financially from afar. The author was not alone in this challenge, and this method of governance turned out not to be sustainable for this organization in a changing world. Several years later, the agency was merged into another organization with more board-friendly meeting hours for working professionals.

The next step for you is to make a meaningful commitment to the organization's annual fund. In a tasteful way, you need to understand its giving pyramid so you can knowledgeably decide where to place yourself. For sleepy organizations, the pyramid may be way behind what other similar organizations have in place. In fact, an appropriate level pledge by you may be a first signal to the board and development office that someone is joining who understands what contemporary board expectations are and that the current board pledging levels are inadequate.

The next step is for you to think carefully about your first initial committee assignments. Your first committee should be one in which you can more deeply understand the mission, its execution, and, in so doing, gain deeper insight to the quality of the operations of the organization. Budgeting, strategic planning, buildings, and grounds are all good committees to get insight on the mission-implementation issues inside the organization. The second committee should be in a role where you will be doing some direct soliciting. A telethon role when you directly solicit previous supporters is an excellent way to start. A person who can grow to do cold-call solicitations effectively is a future development-committee head, capital-campaign-committee head, and maybe even board chair.

I have worked with many effective development committee trustees over the years. I have picked four who collectively demonstrate the broad range of desirable skills. My favorite was Nattie, a former corporate human resource executive before having a family, and who subsequently began engaging heavily in social enterprise organizations. When I first met her, she had a first grader and third grader at a school where I was trustee and chair of the governance committee. Her family had moved into the region a year earlier as a result of her husband's job relocation. Early that fall I got a call from the board chair of her previous school (whom I knew) about her extraordinary work as head of their lower school annual fund. He suggested she might be a good resource for my school's development effort. Within months, she was actively involved in our annual fund and parent chair of one of her children's class. After two years, she was on our board, and co-chair of the annual fund. Her next planned role was to be head of our board development committee. Nattie loved to do cold-call solicitation of new donors. She aimed high (with advice from our development staff), and fearlessly made the targeted ask. More often than not, she succeeded. Sadly, her husband was transferred to another city. In her new location she is again helping her children's new school in the same way. Energetic, fearless, and utterly committed, she set the standard for me.

Susan played a different development committee role than the one I just described. Susan is the absolute connector personified. Her board assignment on an arts organization board first led her to a position on a regional development committee, then the governance committee of the board, and finally the co-head of the corporation. As a member of the regional committee, located near her summer home, she used her network of friends and acquaintances in the region to launch a new gala fundraiser. It has now run three times with ever-greater attendance each time (attended heavily by her friends). You just cannot turn her down. As a member of the governance committee, she is brilliant at spotting appropriate board candidates, getting them to meet other committee members, and fanning their enthusiasm for the organization and its mission. Finally, as head of the newly formed corporation, she helped recruit five or six new corporators. With graciousness she has helped weld the group together. I am always in awe of the breadth of her contacts, and her ability to get them to attend and sponsor events at an organization they did not know very well. Her skill is knowing and liking people. Not surprisingly, she was a successful entrepreneur in a previous career.

A third favorite development person, very different in background from the previous two, is Jason. A highly successful businessman, his son was having a remarkable development experience at a local school. When asked to join the board of the school, after first describing formidable conflicts of both time and a competing board, he turned to the person asking him to join the board and said "Because of what you have done and are doing for my son, I cannot decline this offer." Never missing a board meeting (but attending half the meetings telephonically), he became the lynchpin of the school's redevelopment. Deeply generous with money, time, and contacts, new buildings and new donors came into the school orbit because of him. Construction companies, heavily involved in his company's projects, somehow always got the school's construction work done on time and on budget. Finally, he hosted several large capital campaign launch events at his home. He deeply understands and internalizes the school's mission through the lens of his son's progress. Because of his career, he not only contributes personally in many ways but asks for contributions from others in a way that is really hard to turn down. When an organization has deeply enhanced a child's life, a parent's life, or one's life, a supporter's gratitude can be extraordinary.

Helene taught me a very different lesson. A 65-year-old grandmother, she was on the board of a small K–6th grade school. She was an alumna of the school, as were her two children. Her granddaughter was in second grade. The previous year, the admissions director had turned down her three-year-old grandson for not having enough focus (I guess he didn't do building blocks very well). As chairman of the capital campaign committee, embarrassed by this event, she was the one board member I could not bear to solicit. Somehow sensing my embarrassment, she called me on the telephone after six months on some pretext or another. Guilessly, in the middle of the conversation, she asked me about the project, expressed surprise she had not been solicited, and enquired if I could give her a presentation. Halfway through the presentation, the following night, she stopped me and looking me straight in the eyes and said, "This project makes sense. It will outlive the current head of the school" (whom she held responsible for her grandson being turned down) and gave me a very substantial check, while giving the school he did go to a check 10 times larger. As a final footnote, 13 years later, he was admitted to Harvard College, so the admissions director did not even get the child's potential right. Helene is typical of a type of donor trustee, who is very generous, with great perspective, and loyal to the institution, even if the institution does not always do right by her. You can never get enough of them on a board. Neither do you understand the depth of their commitment until you ask.

Each of these four trustees in very different ways made important contributions to the development structure of their institution. Each was found by the governance committee of their organization, recruited onto the board, and was of value to the organizations in very different ways. Three have been and will be lifelong supporters of their institution long after their terms as trustees expire. The fourth, unfortunately, has moved on geographically and will be difficult to maintain contact with.

Summary

This book is about development. In *Joining a Nonprofit Board: What You Need to Know*,[1] I laid out three roles for the board of trustees:

1. The definition and approval of the organization's mission and the strategy to achieve it.
2. The selection, coaching, and evaluation of the CEO.
3. The securing of the necessary financial resources for the organization.

This book has focused on the third of these roles, the one that social enterprise CEOs repeatedly say consumes 50% of their time. Without funds, mission cannot be fulfilled. Development is the lifeblood of most social enterprises, be they large or small. It is the unique and special responsibility of its trustees and supporters to help secure resources for the organization. These resources are often critical to the organization's success if not survival. There are many ways that individual trustees, given their resources and skill sets, can go about this task. Attracting and harnessing the energies of the right people is key to the long-term success of development.

As I approach this task as a trustee, the key questions I must answer include the following:

---

[1]Marc J. Epstein and F. Warren McFarlan, *Joining a Nonprofit Board: What You Need to Know* (John Wiley & Sons, 2011).

- Do I deeply know, have I internalized and believe in the mission of the organization? Have I developed a five-minute elevator pitch on the topic? Do I use it frequently?

- Am I appropriately personally supportive with both my time and my financial resources on behalf of the enterprise? For most people, we need to give until it hurts and it becomes one of our top two or three philanthropic priorities.

- Do I talk continuously about the organization to the point of driving people around me crazy because of my fixation on its contribution to society?

- Have I introduced the organization and its mission to all the relevant supportive constituencies that I know? Am I prepared to be on the job as a trustee 24/7? One never knows when the opportunity comes to make an appropriate pitch. (One of the author's most successful pitches was made in a chance January encounter on the Boston Common in 0 degree Fahrenheit temperature and driving snow.)

- What things am I particularly good at? Has the development group appropriately harvested these aspects of my skills? Am I good at making the ask? Am I good at making a charismatic speech about the organization? Am I good at creatively using my Rolodex for the benefit of the organization? Each of us has different strengths we can bring to the task.

- What am I not good at today but with practice could do at a satisfactory level? Are there some things that I am so bad at it, it is not worth my improving, but, rather, I should actively avoid these occasions (maybe making a speech is not a core competence of mine)?

- What could I learn to do better that would make me more effective in one or more aspects of development?

- Have I developed a plan about how I can grow as a development-oriented trustee? Have I identified milestones to be passed by certain dates? Have I set personally ambitious development goals? Development is a journey. What must I do to satisfactorily reach the end of the journey?

- Who do I know that would be good at development for my organization? How can I get them involved? Event sponsor, committee member, task force member, creative out-of-the-box thinker, and so forth?
- Can I identify potential development committee members? One must be careful not to rush in this regard. Some people that look good on the surface don't wear well as you get to know them and they get to know your mission. A sour note can do a lot of damage.

Development is the lifeblood of most social enterprises, be they large or small. It is the unique and special responsibility of its trustees and supporters to help secure resources for the organization. These resources are often critical to the organization's success if not survival. There are many ways that individual trustees, given their resources and skill sets, can go about this task. Attracting and harnessing the energies of the right people are key to the long-term success of development.

Bibliography

Burnett, Ken. *Relationship Fundraising*, 2nd ed. Jossey-Bass, 1993.

Craven, Roger. *Retention Fundraising*. Emerson & Church, 2014.

Epstein, Marc, and F. Warren McFarlan. *Joining a Nonprofit Board: What You Need to Know*. Jossey-Bass, 2011.

Greenfield, James. *Fundraising Fundamental: A Guide to Annual Giving for Professional and Volunteers*. John Wiley & Sons, 2002.

Kihlstedt, Andrea. *Asking Styles: Harness Your Personal Fundraising Power*. CharityChannel Press, 2012.

Klein, Kim. *Fundraising for Social Change*, 7th ed. John Wiley & Sons, 2016.

Panas, Jerry. *The Fundraising Habits of Supremely Successful Boards*. Emerson & Church, 2006.

Perry, Richard, and Jeff Schraifels. *It's Not Just About the Money*. Veritus Group, 2014.

Pitman, Marc A. *Ask Without Fear! A Simple Guide to Connecting Donors with What Matters to Them Most*. Executive Books, 2008.

Stevenson, Howard, with Shirley Spence. *Giving to Getting: Fundraising the Entrepreneurial Way*. Timberline, 2011.

Wruck, Craig. *Planned Giving in a Nutshell*, 4th ed. CreateSpace Independent Publishing Platform, 2013.

Index

175